Making the Cat Laugh

Lynne Truss is a writer and broadcaster who started out as a literary editor with a blue pencil and then got sidetracked. The author of the bestselling *Eats, Shoots & Leaves*, she has written three other novels, *Going Loco*, *Tennyson's Gift* and and *With One Lousy Free Packet of Seed*, and numerous radio comedy dramas. Lynne Truss spent six years as the television critic of *The Times*, followed by four (rather peculiar) years as a sports columnist on the same newspaper. She won Columnist of the Year for her work for *Woman's Journal*. She now reviews books for the *Sunday Times* and is a familiar voice on BBC Radio 4. In 2002 she presented *Cutting a Dash*, a well-received Radio 4 series about punctuation ('a sparkling series of essays' – *Daily Telegraph*), which led to the writing of *Eats, Shoots & Leaves*.

Making the Cat Laugh

One Woman's Journal of
Single Life on the Margins

LYNNE TRUSS

PROFILE BOOKS

Published in Great Britain in 2004 by Profile Books
PROFILE BOOKS LTD
58A Hatton Garden
London EC1N 8LX
www.profilebooks.co.uk

Previously published in 1995 by Penguin Books

3 5 7 9 10 8 6 4 2

Typeset in Quadraat by MacGuru Ltd
info@macguru.org.uk

Printed and bound in Great Britain by
Bookmarque Ltd, Croydon, Surrey

A CIP catalogue record for this book is available from the British Library.

ISBN 1 86197 754 9

Contents

Acknowledgements

These columns first appeared in *The Listener*, *The Times* and *Woman's Journal*. At *The Listener*, where I was Literary Editor, Alan Coren encouraged me to start writing a column called 'Margins'; his successor Peter Fiddick was, I think, too scared to stop me. As for the numerous columns from *The Times*, I owe a great debt to Simon Jenkins and Peter Stothard; also Brian MacArthur, Brigid Callaghan, Robert Crampton and Jim McCue. At *Woman's Journal*, Deirdre Vine and Cherry Maslen regularly ring up laughing after receiving my columns. Luckily, this is the desired effect.

This book is a tribute to Kate Jones at Hamish Hamilton, who read all the cuttings I could find, allowed me to laugh like a hyena at my own jokes, and then did all the heavy brainwork. If anyone calls this a scissors-and-paste job, Kate will be very cross. Finally, I must mention Cara Chanteau, formerly of *The Listener*, who warned me in 1987 that if I once became associated professionally with ha-ha jokes about cats there would be no turning back. You were right, Cara. So right.

No Valentines from the cats again. Sometimes I wonder whether they are working as hard at this relationship as I am. Few other pets, I imagine, were lucky enough to find their Valentine's day breakfasts laid out on heart-shaped trays, with the words 'From Guess Who' artfully arranged in Kitbits around the edge. But what do I get in return? Not even a single rose. Not even a 'Charming thought, dear. Must rush.' Just the usual unceremonious leap through the cat-flap; the usual glimpse of the flourished furry backside, with its 'Eat my shorts' connotation. Wearily I sweep up the Kitbits with a dustpan and brush, and try to remember whether King Lear was talking about pets when he coined the phrase about the serpent's tooth.

Of course, the world would be a distinctly different place if cats suddenly comprehended the concept of give and take – if every time you struggled home with a hundredweight of cat food and said accusingly, 'This is all for you, you know,' the kitties accordingly hung their heads and felt embarrassed. Imagine the scene on the garden wall: 'Honestly, guys, I'd love to come out. But the old lady gave me Sheba this morning, and I kind of feel obligated to stay home.' 'She gave you *Sheba*?' 'Yeah. But don't go on about it. I feel bad enough that I can never remember to wipe my feet when I come in from the garden. When I think of how much she does for me ...' (*breaks down in sobs*).

Instead, one takes one's thanks in other ways. For example, take the Valentine's present I bought them: a new cat-nip toy, shaped like a stick of dynamite. This has gone down gratifyingly well, even though the joke misfired slightly. You see, I had fancied the idea of a cat streaking through doorways with a stick of dynamite between its jaws, looking as though it had heroically dived into a threatened mine-shaft and recovered the explosive just in time to save countless lives. In this *Lassie Come Home* fantasy, however, I was disappointed. Instead, cat number one reacted to the dynamite by drooling an alarming quantity of gooey stuff all over it (as though producing ectoplasm), and then hugging it to his chest and trying to kick it to death with his back paws.

Yet all is not lost. If the cat chooses to reject the heroic image, I can still make the best of it. With a few subtle adjustments to my original plan, I can now play a highly amusing game with the other cat which involves shouting, 'Quick! Take cover! Buster's got a stick of dynamite, and we'll all be blown sky-high!' And I dive behind the sofa.

I suppose all this gratitude stuff has been brought to mind because I recently purchased a very expensive cat-accessory, which has somehow failed to elicit huzzahs of appreciation. In fact, it has been completely cold-shouldered. Called a 'cat's cradle', it is a special fleecy-covered cat-hammock which hooks on to a radiator. The cat is suspended in a cocoon of warmth. A brilliant invention, you might think. Any rational cat would jump straight into it. Too stupid to appreciate the full glory of my gift, however, my own cats sleep underneath it (as though it shelters them from rain), and I begin to lose patience.

'Come on, kitties,' I trilled (at first). 'Mmmm,' I rubbed my cheek on the fleecy stuff. 'Isn't this lovely? Wouldn't this make you feel like a – well, er, like an Eastern potentate, or a genie on a magic carpet, or a very fortunate cat having a nice lie-down suspended from a radiator?' However, I stopped this approach after a week of failure. Now I pull on my thick gardening gloves, grab a wriggling cat by the waist, and hold it firmly on its new bed for about forty-five seconds until it breaks away.

I am reminded of a rather inadequate thing that men sometimes say to women, in an attempt to reassure them. The woman says, 'I never know if you love me, Jonathan,' and the man replies smoothly, 'Well, I'm *here*, aren't I?' The sub-text to this corny evasion (which fools nobody) is a very interesting cheat – it suggests that, should the slightest thing be wrong with this man's affections, he would of course push off immediately into the wintry night, rather than spend another minute compromising his integrity at the nice fireside with cups of tea.

Having a cat, I find, makes you susceptible to this line of reasoning – perhaps because it is your only direct line of consolation. 'I wonder if he loves me,' you think occasionally (perhaps as you search the doormat in vain for Valentines with paw-prints on them). And then you gently lift the can-opener from its velvet cushion in the soundproofed kitchen, and with a loud ker-chunk-chunk a cat comes cannoning through the cat-flap, and skids backwards across the lino on its bum. And you think cheerfully, 'Well, of course he does. I mean, he's *here*, isn't he?'

Having now worked at home for just over three weeks, I realize I have broken the longest-ever-period-in-my-life-away-from-the-office barrier, thus confirming that I am definitely not on holiday. So I felt this would be a good time to give any would-be freelancers the benefits of my experience.

1. Advantages:

a) The main advantage of working at home is that you get to find out what cats really do all day. This means they can never again expect you to fall for their 'heavens-what-a-hard-day-I've-had' routine.

b) Also important, you rapidly disabuse yourself of the notion that a novel waits to be written about the fascinating diurnal rhythms of a South London postal district.

c) There is a lot of excitement generated by the arrival of the postman, who delivers lots of press releases and books. Sometimes he chooses not to put a package through the specially enlarged letterbox, but thoughtfully leaves a note telling you to trek three miles to the sorting office to pick it up. Glad of the fresh air, you give thanks for the opportunity to spend a whole morning on a fool's errand. Luckily, the postman never delivers cheques, otherwise you would have to waste a lot of time making boring trips to the bank as well.

d) Where you used to miss good bits on *Start the Week* because you had crashed the car into a BMW on Hyde Park Corner, now you can listen to the whole programme from underneath the duvet. Then you can hear *Money Box*, *Morning Story* and the *Daily Service*. A good programme to get out of bed to is *The World at One*. Within a week, the metaphorical lark gives up waiting for you, and rises unaccompanied.

e) Where you used to do the shopping once a month, and buy 10lb bags of frozen rissoles, now you learn that you can visit the same corner-shop five times in a single day before the proprietor gets suspicious and starts following you around.

2. Disadvantages:

a) Cats don't talk very much, and if you ask one to 'copy-taste' a piece you have written, he will probably sit on it with his back to you.

b) Whenever serious work is contemplated, the words 'Time

for a little something' spring immediately to mind; ditto the words 'There's no point carrying on when you're tired, is there?', and 'They can probably wait another day for this, actually.'

c) When you read your pieces in print, the key sentence has always been cut, and the best joke ruined by a misprint. But when you run along to the newsagent's to amend all remaining copies, the shopkeeper – recognizing you from 1(e) – is unsympathetic. 'Why don't you get yourself a proper job?' he says. 'The trouble with you is you've too much time on your hands.'

Single Bananas

An old friend of mine, who five years ago migrated to the country with her husband to propagate children and rear a garden, recently sent me a card which I didn't know quite how to take. 'Wishing you all good luck', she wrote, 'on your chosen path.' I sat looking at it with my fingers in my mouth. What did she mean, exactly, by this notion of the 'chosen path'? I assumed she meant it kindly, but it made me feel suddenly exposed and distant. Hey, where did everybody go? Supposing that she imagined herself on a path radically divergent from mine, I instantly pictured myself labouring alone up a narrow, steep, dusty, brambly trail with a determined look on my face, as though illustrating a modern-day parable about the grim sacrifices of feminism.

So vivid was this picture, in fact, that I could feel the stinging nettles brushing against my legs. It was awful. I felt thirsty; my head swam; the sun scorched my shoulders. Looking down, I observed my friend ambling happily in the sunshine on a broad level path with a pram and husband, while small apple-cheeked children ran off to right and left, frolicking with lambs. I would have watched for longer, but a bloke called Bunyan came along and told me to hop it.

But I was definitely confused by the notion of the chosen

path, and dwelt on it for days. Did I *choose* this, then? And if so, why couldn't I remember doing it? Hadn't I always thought, rather naïvely, that there was still time to make these decisions about wife-and-motherhood in the future – that the cross-roads were just over the horizon? But it turns out that the last exit was miles back, and I am a person whose chosen path speaks for itself. The hardest part was realizing I can never be a teenage tennis phenomenon. How on earth did I let things drift so badly?

For some reason I thought of the careers mistress at school – perhaps because she represents the single point in my life when I recognized a T-junction and made a definite choice. She wanted us all to be nurses, you see; and I refused. Brainy sixth-formers would queue at the careers office with fancy ideas about Oxford and Cambridge and archaeology, and come out again 15 seconds later, waving nursing application forms and looking baffled. 'You have to have A-levels to be a nurse now, you know, Miss Hoity-Toity!' she would bark after them, twitching.

At my age, women are supposed to hear the loud ticking of a biological clock, but I think I must have bought the wrong battery for mine. The only time I experienced the classic symptoms was when I desperately wanted a car. It was weird. If I spotted another woman driving a Peugeot 205, I would burst into tears. In the end, friends tactfully stopped mention-ing their cars in my presence ('My Volvo did *such* a funny thing the other day – oh Lynne, how awful. I didn't see you'). And there was that one shameful occasion when I lurked outside a supermarket half-considering snatching a Metro. 'What a lovely bonnet you've got,' I whispered, fingering it lightly. But then a woman shouted 'Oi!', so I picked up my string bag and scarpered.

Now I realize that what I want is a book. So much do I want to give birth to a book that I experience 'false alarms' – when

I think I am 'with book', but am not really. Once a month I phone up my agent and say, 'It's happening!' And she says, 'How marvellous!' And then I have to ring again a week later and say, 'Bad news,' and she says, 'Never mind, conception is a mysterious thing.' I suddenly realize that a book would be a comfort in my old age, and I try to ignore the argument that there are already too many books in the world competing for the available shelf-space. Mine, of course, will be a poor fatherless mite, but I shall love it all the more for that.

Perhaps the image of the paths and crossroads is just the wrong one. Perhaps I did always know where I wanted to go, but just walked backwards with my eyes closed, pretending there was no act of will involved. Because I do recall from early youth that while other children pleaded with their mums for miniature bridal outfits and little dolls that went wee-wees, I was campaigning for a brick- built Wendy House in the garden where I could lock the door and sit at an enormous typewriter. My only imaginary friends were phantom insurance collectors, a person from Porlock and the printer's boy.

My idea of a Wendy House was a rather grandiose one, I suppose. It involved guttering and utilities and a mantelpiece where I could put the rent money, not to mention trouble with the drains. I remember when a little friend told me she had acquired a Wendy House, and I was wild with envy. But when I went to see it, it was just a canvas job with painted-on windows. Fancy telling a gullible kid that this was a Wendy House. Sometimes I wonder what happened when she eventually uncovered the deception. Probably she married somebody with a big house and had lots of kids in double-quick time, to establish a sense of security. In which case, I wish her all good luck on her chosen path.

The prevailing notion of the lone woman traveller seems to have been fixed about a century ago, and entails such heart-stopping intrepidity and pluck that there is not much in our banal modern lives to touch it. I mean, compared with the achievement of striding across the Andes armed only with a pocket bible and a big stick, the modern-day purchase of an air ticket to Los Angeles is going to look rather paltry, isn't it? And compared with Amelia Earhart flying solo across the Atlantic in a rattling crate with nothing but a soup Thermos and a star-map, the modern woman's stout-hearted endurance of an eleven-hour scheduled flight (complete with movies and drinks) is emphatically nothing to write home about.

Intrepidity is relative, however. To me, the acme of being brave is catching a bus in central London after 9pm, or enduring a whole instalment of *Just a Minute* on Radio 4. So it was only natural that when I booked my single ticket to LA before Christmas I was so transported by my own pluckiness that for a moment I thought I smelled quinine and hartshorn in the air. Sod Amelia Earhart's soup, I thought; this feels *great*. How brave and adventurous I am, to travel alone! I nearly phoned up Maria Aitken to suggest she make a documentary.

This was the first thing I learnt about solitary travel, by the way: that the habit of tiresome (and bogus) self-congratulation starts at the ticket desk and never wears off. 'Hey, I made it!' you say proudly, as you step off the plane, having done nothing more heroic during the flight than stumble to the loo a couple of times. 'Wow, I collected my luggage from the carousel! I found my hotel! I had some M&Ms from the mini-bar! I turned on the TV and it worked!' This exclamatory tone is a bit relentless, I'm afraid. 'I hired a car! I looked someone up in the telephone directory! I ate a bagel in Santa Barbara!' And so on.

Travelling *à deux* does not encompass this splendid sense of perpetual infantile achievement; I don't know why. Travelling *à deux*, in fact, is generally a much more sober and grown-up affair, with precision map-reading not only its greatest measure of success but also (alas) its highest goal.

'Nicely map-read, dear,' says the driver, calmly applying the handbrake.

'Well, thanks very much. It got a bit tricky around Nuneaton, but I think I kept my head.'

'We didn't get lost at all, did we?'

'No, we didn't.'

The advantages to travelling alone are many, as I discovered. For one thing, you can listen to old Beach Boys hits on the car radio without your passenger huffily twiddling with FM to find something else. Secondly, you can take art galleries at your own pace (at a brisk roller-skating speed, if preferred) without feeling guilty. Thirdly, you can browse in shops without first devising an hour's alternative entertainment for your companion (who will otherwise stand next to the door looking helpless, like a tethered puppy). And fourthly, you can choose a route for your journey without your companion suddenly spotting a scenic wiggly detour just a few miles short of your destination.

The main disadvantage – as I also discovered – is that when travelling on fast roads at night it is impossible to drive and navigate at the same time. Something to do with the number of hands, I think. Consequently, on a simple trip across town to Pasadena, you can get so deeply lost on the freeway system that you think the night will swallow you up (just like poor old Amelia Earhart) and that your cats at home will die of broken hearts waiting for your return. Such terrors are feeble, no doubt, compared with those of the stout Victorian lady wandering lost in the deserts of Arabia, describing huge ragged circles in the shifting sands. But I can assure you that the cry 'I don't want to go to Glendale!' represents the nearest I have ever got to a nervous breakdown.

Perhaps map-reading really is what holidays are about – strenuously mastering streetplans, so that one can always find the route back to the bus station. I admit that maps obsess me; as a founder member of Cartomaniacs Anonymous, I resent and refute the theory that women are genetically incapable of reading maps (although I rather like the notion of dangling a copy of the London A–Z over a pregnant woman, to determine the gender of the unborn child. If the foetus shrugs and turns its back, murmuring 'Ach, I'm sure you'll find it,' it is probably a boy.)

So no wonder my night of terror in Los Angeles made such an impression on me: every time I braked abruptly at the sight of yet another freeway approach, all my maps slid off the passenger seat on to the floor. Moreover, when I reached inside the glove compartment for hartshorn, there was never any there. *Alone and Disoriented Without a Smelling Bottle in Glendale.* Perhaps I should make the call to Maria Aitken, after all.

An old chum, newly spliced, recently invited me to dinner in his new marital home. Ordinarily I would have said yes automatically, but this time I heard myself imposing conditions.

'Is it a nice house?' I asked.

'Yes, very nice.'

'And you and your new wife are really happy there?'

'Yes, we are.'

'With a nice well-organized kitchen, and a big fireplace, and a patio for barbecues, and a little room suitable for Baby?'

'Yeah, sort of.'

'Well, in that case the answer's no.'

There was an awkward pause.

'Did you say no?'

'That's right,' I said briskly. 'Not in a million years. Let's meet at Leicester Square for a pizza or something instead. Then we can eat and talk just the same, but afterwards I can come home feeling quite all right and not mysteriously depressed because your home life is so lovely. All right?'

If he was surprised by this outburst, so was I. I had no idea I felt so strongly. All I knew was that sometimes, after a delight-ful evening spent with perfect hosts in a full, groaning family house, a single person spends the next few days dumb with misery, hating everybody, and bursting into unexpected tears during heart-warming re-runs of *Flipper*. I confessed my 'Not in a million years' speech to a friend, who said she understood, and who mentioned that at least I had been assertive without being aggressive. Which made me bloody annoyed. 'What's the point of that?' I yelled. Damn. Next time, I shall shout 'Sod your fancy house with its bloody patio and its baby room, you make me sick, you people.' Because there are times when a sub-text simply won't do.

The alternative strategies to an outright No Thanks – though possibly better etiquette in the strict sense – are too wearisome to contemplate. For example, you can accept the invitation, and then half an hour before arrival phone up with a fabricated story about a last-minute mercy-dash ('I'm so sorry, but if I don't deliver this jar of rollmop herrings to the Foreign Office in the next hour, we could find ourselves at war with Finland!'). But is this less rude than explaining your true feelings? I think not. Worst of all, surely, is to agree to come, turn up punctually, make perfect-guest 'Ooh lovely' noises at the wallpaper, and then sever your wrist quietly in their nice big kitchen while pretending to help with the puddings.

Don't get me wrong. Things get better for single people every day. Oh yes. How cheerful to reflect, for example, that Sainsburys now sells 'Single Bananas' in a special bag. But we are not the norm, despite our bananas. We are seen as some-thing akin to the rogue animals in wildlife films, the ones that are tolerated by the herd but don't fit in, and are photographed sulking hundreds of yards off, snuffling in long white grass. When lone dolphins turn up in British harbours (clearly enjoying a walloping good time eating fresh salmon and frolicking with the boats), the British public invariably feels sorry for them, and worries about finding them a suitable mate. It is the same benevolent but mistaken instinct that makes married people invite you to their new house.

What nobody appreciates, of course, is that the poor old dolphin fields invitations all day, through his ultrasonic mindwaves. 'Come to dinner, we haven't seen you in ages,' he hears from a happy nuclear dolphin family five miles out to sea. 'Bugger,' thinks the dolphin, wishing he had remembered to switch on his answering machine. How can he say he moved five miles (and risked having to swim with New Age poets in wet-suits) just to escape all this? Treading water for a minute, he programs his super-brain to run through the available strategies, and instantly feels doubly depressed. Pizzas in Leicester Square is not a viable option for a dolphin; and the rollmop herrings routine cuts no ice whatever in a marine context.

He is caught all ways actually, because he can't be assertive or aggressive, since neither is in his nature. And he *always* finds Flipper depressing. What a bind. So in the end, he agrees to visit, swims miles, has a marvellous time, adores the kids, applauds the bold choice of murky green throughout, gets home late, and flops out exhausted with a smile on his face. And then, for about a week later, he mopes miserably in the water, and everyone says it must be because he misses the company of other dolphins.

Perhaps it is a phase you go through, this ugly envy stuff. I hope so, certainly. I know one woman who is perfectly all right most of the time, but who bursts into tears every time she gets a wedding invitation, so that we have to rush out and have a pizza at Leicester Square, where we talk bravely about single bananas. Edna Ferber said that single life, like drowning, is a delightful sensation once you cease to struggle – but is this comforting, or isn't it? The analogy isn't bad, certainly: your whole life unfolds before your eyes, and you entertain strange dreamy consoling thoughts such as 'I shall never have to wash my hair again, anyway.' Meanwhile, however, you can't help wishing that those nice married people on the bank would stop chucking you lifebelts, so that you can just get on with it.

⌒

I went to see *Batman Returns* last week. A man-friend had dropped the offhand remark that the Michelle Pfeiffer character had reminded him of me, so naturally I couldn't wait to find out what he meant. After all, Michelle Pfeiffer and I are seldom mentioned in the same breath; and on the evidence of the publicity shots of Catwoman – the sexy patent leather cat-suit, the high heels, whip, and hood with little black ears – I have to admit I was chuffed and flattered.

As I stood in the ticket queue at Leicester Square I preened myself by licking the back of my hand and rubbing my forehead with it. I flexed my painted claws. Meeeeow, I thought. How perceptive of this male acquaintance to realize that while I portray myself in this column as a frowzy, spinsterish stay-at-home, in reality I am a lithe, crazy, dangerous feline-type animal who prowls the moonlit rooftops after dark, purring to the sounds of the night-time city.

But alas, no sooner was I embarked on my second vat of popcorn than I noticed that the Michelle Pfeiffer character in *Batman Returns* is a frowzy, spinsterish stay-at-home, instantly recognizable as Single Life material at its most abject and pitiable. Damn. Her name is Selina. Each evening she bursts into her apartment with a ritualistic shout of 'Honey, I'm home!' followed by 'Oh I forgot, I'm not married.' She kicks off her shoes, listens to the answering machine, pours milk for the cat, talks aimlessly to herself. Evidently it was Selina, not Catwoman, that my friend had been talking about. I put my head in my popcorn tub for a moment, and screamed with the minimum disruption.

No wonder Selina escapes this paltry existence by assuming the identity of Catwoman ('I am Catwoman, hear me roar'). It is a sensible decision. The only problem is that, before it can happen, she must suffer a brutal death from defenestration – which gives pause to all the would-be Catwomen in the audience who are fed up with shouting 'Honey, I'm home' to an empty flat. I mean, is it worth chucking yourself off the Shell building on the remote chance it might turn you into Catwoman? Well, it's tricky. I am still weighing it up.

But if it boils down to clothes, I am sunk. You see, in order to become Catwoman it is important that you can rummage in your wardrobe for an old patent leather coat; you then rip its seams and magically re-fashion it into the appropriate figure-hugging costume. Imagine your disappointment, then, if having flung yourself from a high roof (and become a glassy-eyed un-dead) you opened your closet, snapping your expectant pinking shears, to find only a brown calf-length fun-fur, with no patent leather in sight. You would have to become Teddywoman instead, and it would not be the same.

'I am Teddywoman, hear me not make any aggressive noise,' you would say lamely, as you sat with your arms out in front of you, unable to bend your elbows. It would be dreadful. While chaos overtook your city, you would just sit there looking stiff and fluffy and hoping that your eyeballs didn't fall out. There would be no opportunity for Batman to fall in love with you during exciting bouts of single combat, either. At best, he might pick you up by the ear and trail you on the ground behind him. And admit it, this would make you feel quite stupid.

I don't suppose Batman's creators needed to think very

hard about the animal identity of his female counterpart. Dogwoman would not draw much male interest. Spiderwoman has been done before. Elephantwoman would look like a rip-off. And Ferretwoman is too suggestive. So Catwoman was the obvious answer. However, lots of potential kitty-joke plot-devices were disappointingly left untapped by *Batman Returns*. For example, just as Batman is summoned across Gotham City by a special Bat-design searchlight shone on to solid cloud, couldn't Catwoman have been summoned from miles distant by the shaking of a little box of Miaow-mix?

I liked *Batman Returns*. The one thing that really worried me, though, was the role of the Gotham City populace, who are required repeatedly to turn up in grey hats and coats for Yuletide speeches outside the City Hall. Each time they do this, a dastardly attack is launched against them, entailing multiple explosions, car chases, punch-ups and deaths. At one point, this passive crowd is sprayed with machine-gun fire from a trick umbrella. So why on earth do they keep turning out, these people? Imagine, if you lived in Gotham City, and somebody said 'Are you coming to hear the new mayor address us this evening?', wouldn't you pause momentarily before limping off to another apocalyptic pasting? A twinge of pain from your latest shrapnel wounds would surely nudge your decision one way or the other.

I suppose one should not be surprised. Only a city of fools relies on a man in a bat-costume to protect it from evil. But perhaps the Gothamites deliberately expose themselves to extreme danger in the hope that they will be transformed, like Michelle Pfeiffer, into a new superhuman chimera. In which case, you have to admire their pluck. The only trouble is, you can't imagine a movie called *Lemmingman*, can you?

The bit that always stops me dead is where it says 'Photo appreciated'. Up to then I am fine, almost excited. I can even entertain the pathetic notion that I am being singled out personally.

'Intellectual Andre Agassi lookalike with steady job' (it says) 'seeks lonely cat-fixated Teddywoman for evenings of mutual squeaks. Extensive knowledge of *EastEnders* an advantage. My dream lady has clean TV licence, an interest in the fashion potential of household fluff, and a Jeff Bridges video collection. Please write to Box 213. Oh, and I nearly forgot. Photo appreciated.'

'Damn,' I yell, and head-butt the bath-taps. Bleeding from the brow, I stab wildly at the Lonely Hearts column, speechless with frustration. There he is! Mister Dreamboat himself! But he wants a photo! And now we can never meet because I don't have any pictures. What a personal disaster. 'Perhaps you could send your Single Life picture?' ventures a passing cat, sort-of telepathically. 'Hah!' I shout. 'How can I send a newspaper clipping, you fur-faced poltroon! Besides, this picture gives most people the impression I am 93!'

I clamber from the bath, press a towel to my head, and go through the usual frantic motions of searching the flat for a suitable picture. But while I rifle my home with all the gusto of the professional burglar, I know there is no chance whatever of success. In the end, in desperation, I grab my passport and some pinking shears and tussle with the temptation to cut out the picture forthwith. But luckily I remember in the nick of time that a) it was taken seven years ago; and b) some of the proffered squeaking might take place abroad.

Sinking on the debris, I sob quietly. If I say I always look lousy in photographs, there is one large, obvious inference which I would naturally rather not contemplate. But there is another reason, honestly, for my despondence. It is that I find it really hard to pose. In front of a camera I just smile in a 'this is it, there's no more' kind of way, and trust that 'being myself' will do the job. This is utterly wrong-headed, of course, because for a successful photo you must seize the moment, choose your statement, and go for it. Whereas I invariably look as though the statement I have chosen is 'I am simple-minded. Please don't mind me. Children are safe.'

For this reason, book jackets depress me. I am amazed by the intensely serious faces adopted by authors on the backs of books. It is as though they have been subjected to some weird voodoo practice, where all the personality and humour has been pulled out in strings through their nostrils. Look at the pictures of the Booker shortlist people (the men, anyway) and you will see they seem to have memorized a list of permitted authorial qualities – a list that is unfortunately rather short. It goes: Brainy, Moody, Mad, Sincere, Sensitive, Anxious, Supercilious, Dangerous, Grumpy. On this list, you will observe, Harmless is notable by its absence.

Evidently authors may choose three (not more) of these qualities and put them together in subtle combinations. Thus, taking a random selection from the bookshelves, one finds that the Ian McEwan of *Black Dogs*, say, has opted for brainy, anxious and mad; that Martin Amis, formerly brainy, supercilious and dangerous (*London Fields*), has now daringly regrouped as brainy, sincere and anxious (*Time's Arrow*). And Nigel Williams (*They Came from SW19*) has achieved an amazing triple – of brainily sensitive, sincerely sensitive and sensitively grumpy.

For women the range is smaller and doesn't include Brainy. That's just the way it is. Traditionally women could choose from Clever, Nice, Shiny, Well Made-up and Pet-owning, but usually said to hell with it and took the lot. To this list a few new elements have been added recently. For example, Jeanette Winterson (famously self-effacing author of *Written on the Body*) has added Challenging, Bloody-Minded and

Eyes that Follow You Around the Room. Pictures of women authors sometimes have a verge-of-tears quality, reminiscent of Julia Margaret Cameron's famous picture *Despair*, which was achieved by locking the juvenile sitter in a cupboard for a couple of hours beforehand. Jeanette Winterson does not look like someone recently emerged from a cupboard. She does, however, resemble a person who has just locked someone else in a cupboard, and put the key down the lav.

Meanwhile, what do I do about the Andre Agassi man? If I don't send a picture, he will smell a rat. Perhaps I should get a heap of coins and take residence in a Photo-Me booth for the afternoon, trying out statements. Think moody. Think mad. Think grumpy. But what I don't understand is this. Given that the mad, brainy, sincere look is only a pretence, why not go for something a bit more dramatic? Such as Livid, Amnesiac, Paranoid, or Escaping from Wolves? Unfortunately I shall have to settle for Concussed by Bathroom Appliance. Which probably means that my photo won't be appreciated very much, after all.

A man friend who lives in California recently phoned me at great expense from a Santa Barbara call-box and asked me what clothes I had on. Not having read any fashionable American novels about sex-by-phone, I found this rather unsettling. It came out of the blue. I mean, we observed the usual preliminary greetings, such as 'What time is it where you are?' and 'Have you seen *The Player* yet, isn't it great?' But we had barely touched on the elections and the earthquake forecasts before he posed this extraordinary question about my attire, leaving me all perplexed and wrong-footed.

Was this a dirty phone-call, I thought, or was he simply concerned to conjure up an innocent mental picture of his faraway pal? Should I give him the benefit of the doubt? Playing for time (and angling for clues) I asked what *he* was wearing, but his answer didn't help. Evidently his outfit consisted of a T-shirt and trousers, some trainers and a beany hat. 'Sounds very nice,' I said non-committally, wondering whether the beany hat was a code for something. Either way, I was still completely in the dark about whether to confess to the old grey army socks and the jumbo dungarees.

Fran Lebowitz once said that the telephone is a good way to talk to people without having to offer them a drink. Personally, I see it as a good way of talking to people without having to dress up in a high-cut Kim Basinger costume, or apologize for your paltry wardrobe of seductive gear. In the end, I decided to ignore the overtones, and acted dumb. I said that actually my clothes were so thickly matted with cat-hair and household fluff that I could no longer identify them with any confidence. A smart evasion, which seemed to do the trick, because the subject turned to the Richter scale forthwith.

I was more disturbed by this conversation than it really merited, perhaps. But I hold the telephone in reverence as an instrument of pure verbal communication, and I don't like to see it messed about. Surely this is the only form of talk in which you can convince yourself that the other person is really engaged in a flow of words entirely undistracted by the extraneous. Which is precisely why it always comes as a shock to discover that for the past ten minutes the other person has been keeping an eye on *Northern Exposure*, or marking exams, fitting a new flea-collar on a resistant pet, or reading a funny bit from *Tristram Shandy*.

Saying 'Have I caught you at a bad time?' does not eliminate this problem, I find.

YOU: Have I caught you at a bad time?

THEM: No, not at all. How are things? (*Tap, tap, tap.*)

YOU: Are you sure you're not busy?

THEM: (*Tap, tap, tap.*) What?

YOU: Listen, I'll phone another time.

THEM: No, really. This is lovely. (*Tap, tap, tap.*)

YOU: Look, are you typing, or something?

THEM: Just the radio play. (*Tap, tap, tap.*) The one about existential despair. (*Tap, tap, tap.*) I'm doing this big speech about the black void of silence and the sensation (*tap, tap, tap*) that nobody is listening, anywhere in the universe (*tap, tap, tap*) to anyone else. I don't mind if you want to talk, though. (*Tap, tap, tap.*) It doesn't bother me.

YOU: I'm surprised you can write and talk at the same time.

THEM: Perhaps you're right. I'll stop for a while. (*Clank, clatter, tinkle.*)

YOU: What's that?

THEM: Nothing much. I thought I'd start dinner.

The worst thing is when they don't mention they have guests. You chatter away for twenty minutes or so, and then hear them whisper, 'Go ahead without me. I think she just needed someone to talk to. Sorry.' That's the other illusion of the telephone, of course: that the other person is on their own, just as you are. There is a woman I know who answers the phone in your presence and signals at you to wait; and then she talks animatedly for thirty minutes without giving a single indication to the person on the other end that there is any reason not to. Meanwhile she pulls faces at you, mimes 'nearly finished' repeatedly, and makes exaggerated comic pleading gestures when you make embarrassed efforts to leave. Imagine how awkward one feels phoning her up, after witnessing all that.

Perhaps I worried too much about my American friend's innocent question. He only asked what I was wearing, after all. He didn't ask if I was entertaining a coach party from the Midlands, or examining A-levels, or making a casserole; whereas in fact I was doing all three, as well as finishing my script for the epic *Night of the Living Teddywomen* and practising bird-calls.

Funny he didn't remark on the array of sound effects, really – *Shsh, tick, chop, tap, cuckoo* – (something like a jaunty clock repair shop in a Disney cartoon). But then perhaps he was simply transported by the unbearably erotic notion of a woman, six thousand miles away, dressed up to resemble the inside of a Hoover bag.

~

When you are a single person, the world is full of happy couples. That's the idea, anyway; the tragic little myth we have all picked up from somewhere. In this version of events, life is a couples-only ceilidh in which the single person is the perpetual wallflower; she leans over the bridge in St James's Park in her lonely anorak, crooning the plaintive country song from *Starlight Express* ('I've been U-n-c-o-u-p-l-e-d'), while happy newlyweds chuck beach-balls about, and giggle together at the ducks.

This is all rubbish, of course. It rubs no salt in my wound to see people happily paired off; they could waltz around the concourse at Waterloo in their dozens, and I wouldn't care. No, what single life means to me (strangely enough) is that I can't stand to hear couples bickering about where to park the car; or stalking off in a huff at the supermarket. It seems terrible. The other day I saw a man in the street trying repeatedly to take his wife's hand, and she kept snatching it away again. It made my blood run cold, like watching somebody kick a dog.

I wonder whether people parade their marital misery because they are proud of it. At traffic lights, you can always see couples in cars staring out in different directions with their mouths set rectangular like letter-boxes, and with a small thundercloud visible above their heads. You will have noticed also how those cheerful 'Bob and Sandy' windscreen stickers have largely disappeared, which is something I take personal credit for. I kept knocking on the glass and saying, 'Hey, cheer up, Bob, you've got Sandy,' and 'Cheer up, Sandy, you've got Bob,' until they took the stupid things down and cut them in half.

So if I tend to avoid dinner parties, it is not because I am afraid the couples will canoodle in front of me, but because the couplesome strangers Derek and Jo need only exchange a private hostile glance over the sage derby and I start to panic on their behalf. It is not happy, this Derek-and-Jo; it will split up; its Derek-and-Jo kiddies will suffer. I turn into a kind of Cassandra, prophesying the sooner-or-later catastrophe of Derek-and-Jo with a forlorn certainty, usually even before they have reached the front gate and started arguing.

It is a heavy burden: to see the inevitable with such clarity. 'See the cracks!' I moan inwardly (after some ritual 'who's driving?' fracas after pudding). 'Oh, woe! Hear the marital fabric split and rend, stitch by stitch verily from top to bottom! Weep, ye marrieds! Weep!' It is an odd way to behave in a Crouch End dining room, but of course nobody listens anyway. Or if they do, they probably put it down to personal disappointment.

This fatalism seems to be the worst aspect of being single; it gives you a cranky view of the world. You have heard of ex-hippies who advocate trepanning as the answer to everything (drill a hole in your skull to let off steam)? Well, I am quite similar, only I think everyone must tear up the marriage lines or sell the double bed, or *for heaven's sake quit moaning*. As you can imagine, this makes me pretty useless as an adviser when relationships hit stormy seas, since my suggestions are always equally radical and precisely the same.

'I think he's seeing another woman, but I can't believe it's true,' sobs a friend, desperate for support. 'Split up,' I advise, promptly, 'and make sure you get the tumble drier.' 'I am in such turmoil,' says another. 'My wife wants to have a baby and the idea makes me dream about being eaten alive by a big hairy mouth with teeth in it.' 'Mmm,' I say thoughtfully. 'Have you considered going your separate ways?' On Radio 4's comedy news programme *On the Hour* the other day, I heard: 'A palace spokesman has today confirmed that Prince Harry is to split up,' and I automatically thought 'Good idea; best thing' before seeing the joke.

The thing is, coupledom is a bit like childbirth; a week after it's finished, you can't imagine what it was like, or how you got into it. This is the gulf between single people and couples, and between the different bits of one's own life. One minute you are Derek-and-Jo; the next you are Derek *or* Jo. And in each state you can't imagine the other. I have spent about 80 per cent of my adult life in proper committed long-term relationships, yet at the moment all I can clearly remember is that I once startled my boyfriend by asking, out of the blue: 'Why aren't you a pony?'

This 'Why don't they split up?' syndrome is not sour grapes, I promise. It is not even cynicism. It is just an unanswerable point of view, similar to a religious conviction. The only trouble with this particular panacea (like trepanning) is that once you have done it, you can't do it again. Consequently its evangelists cannot follow their own advice. What do trepanners do when they are depressed? If they kept drilling holes in their heads, they would risk being mistaken for patio strawberry-planters.

Similarly, once you have split up you can't keep doing it, unless of course you are a simple organism like an amoeba. So it is quite ironic, really. Here I am, advocating the new revolutionary pluck-it-out, cut-and-run approach to personal happiness, while at home I am gradually learning how to patch things up.

One of the more difficult things to accept about being newly single is that there is no one to strike chore-bargains with. You know the sort of thing: 'If you do the breakfast, I'll take the bin out'; 'I'll get the milk, you get the papers.' Make such fair's-fair suggestions to a cat, I find, and it will just look preoccupied, and suddenly remember an urgent appointment outside.

The beauty of efficient teamwork is that it cuts through the grease and grime of household activity with a brisk one-two, reminiscent of the old telly adverts for Flash. Wisshh, woossshh, all done. 'You make a cup of tea, while I lie full-out on this sofa, preventing it from bucking up and killing somebody.'

Jobs that can't be tackled simultaneously stretch out instead in long miserable single file, like prisoners on a chain-gang, and are dealt with on the weary principle of one-damn-thing-after-another. The plodding linear quality is depressing. Sometimes you forget, of course, and glance optimistically at the bin, fleetingly wondering whether someone else has taken out the rubbish. But they usually have not. The cheerful midnight pixie with bucket and mop is a sweet and potent myth, but it is cruelly misleading.

Looking on the bright side, however, there is great consolation in the knowledge that the Mr Nobody who takes out the bin is also the Mr Nobody who moves things around so that you can't find them. Take the TV remote control, for example. In my old cohabiting days, how many times did I search frantically among sofa cushions for it, knowing in my heavy heart that it was probably travelling anti-clockwise on the M25 by now, snug in a coat pocket on the back seat of the boyfriend's car? Living alone, then, it is no wonder you rejoice that things remain precisely where you left them. You feel a great warmth inside on the day you realize that *if you haven't finished the marmalade, there is still some marmalade left*. The only interference I have experienced since living alone was when I emerged from the bath one day to discover the word 'trhjwqxz' on my otherwise blank word-processor screen. I gulped, and stood stock still for a minute, feeling the pulse race in my neck. And then I realized that a cat had made a dash across the keyboard.

I mention all this because last week I left a friend alone in my flat for a couple of hours, and when I came back I realized I could retrace virtually every moment of his stay, just by observing all the things he had moved from their usual places. The loo seat was up. A plate with toast crumbs awaited me on the draining-board, along with a knife tinged with Marmite. A couple of inches of wine had gone from an opened bottle, and a glass with dregs in it was rolling on the living-room floor. A book had been replaced in the wrong position on a shelf, a window opened (and not closed again), the backdoor key hidden so successfully it took me two hours to find it. I moved stealthily around the flat, feeling a bit like Sherlock Holmes on the trail of exotic cigar-ash. 'He's been *here*, too!' I whispered excitedly. 'See, he has moved these cassettes!' Thank goodness I didn't have a magnifying-glass, or I would have been down on the carpet, observing the pile for footprints.

I felt proud and irritated in equal measure: proud that I can now (like Holmes himself) detect the tiniest variation in the depth of dust on a pile of *Radio Times*; irritated for obvious reasons (mainly to do with washing up). But there was something rather macabre about this Do Your Own Forensics activity, and eventually I stopped thinking about it. The idea of living alone is somehow quite closely associated with the idea of dying alone, too; and I didn't want to think about the giveaway clues packed into my own day-to-day life. 'We found a half-eaten jar of pickled onions next to the bath. She had fed the cats but not washed the spoon. A little Post-It note was attached to the bin, with the mysterious words "I suppose it's my turn again?" written on it in big wobbly capital letters, underlined.'

If this sounds self-pitying and morbid, it is nevertheless something that single people very often joke about; the collective single mind contains a whole sub-section labelled: 'What if I died?' 'Thanks for the present,' they say, 'but what if I died, and somebody found the room stacked to shoulder height with twenty-five years' worth of *Pet Fish Monthly*?' I remember a woman once proudly describing to me how she had rescued herself from acute self-consciousness by assembling a library of pop psychology books, with titles such as 101 *Ways Not To Care What Other People Think*. The effect of these books had been miraculous she said; she had been transformed into someone who did not give a damn. I was impressed, and asked her to check the publishing details. 'Oh, but I threw them all out, in the end,' she said in a lowered voice. 'I mean, what if I died and people came in and found a load of books with titles like those?'

❧

The day that I became single again – some time last August – I felt it was important to perform some symbolic acts. After all, I reasoned, you never know when a social anthropologist might be watching. I tried to picture what a newly single woman would be expected to do, to mark the reclaiming of the living environment after years of cohabitation. Washing the walls and beating the carpets sounded the right kind of thing – but on the other hand it also sounded a bit strenuous, and I didn't want to alarm the cats.

So perhaps, instead, the newly single woman might do a little light tidying? Form the old newspapers into distinct new piles? Pick up the dusty used tissue that she always stared at, mindlessly, through hour-long telephone conversations? This all seemed manageable, given the emotional circumstances. Oh yes, and she might ceremoniously replace the lavatory seat to its 'down' position, with an exaggerated flourish and a round of applause. This was ample *Coming of Age in Samoa* stuff for a single afternoon.

But I remember that the first evening I was also moved to root through a heap of books until I found Anthony Storr's *Solitude*. This was a book I had wanted to read for a very long time; and I felt I should seize the moment. I read it avidly until 9.30pm, after which I left it unopened on the coffee table for the next three months, hoping that some of its inspiring message would miraculously buoy my spirit. I don't know why I stopped reading. People must have thought I was a real stoic, savouring a book called *Solitude* over such a long period. Either that, of course, or that I couldn't read without moving my lips.

Storr thinks that solitude has much to recommend it. He says it promotes creativity – making people write novels, and so forth. Look at Anita Brookner, Edward Gibbon and, er, many, many others. Interestingly, a large proportion of our philosophers turn out to have been lonely miserable gits who walked about wearing buckets on their heads.

There was something wrong with the appeal of this argument, but I couldn't put my finger on it. Months later, however, I do still hold out hope that the novel-writing and world-class philosophy stage will bounce along nicely when the time is right. I have bought a few note-pads, just in case. And a cardigan. The only trouble is that at the moment I can't seem to pass a rather more mundane stage in the experience of solitude. I can't seem to overcome my excitement at being able (at long last) to listen to *The Archers* without having to do it in the shed.

I never accepted the idea that 'love means never having to

say you're sorry'. In my own case, love invariably means never being allowed to listen to The Archers – and in fact saying 'Oops, sorry, I'll turn it off then, shall I?' when discovered in the guilty act. I kept faith with The Archers during three solid years of strict prohibition, just waiting for the day when I could again turn the theme tune up to maximum volume, as a statement: 'Yes, I love The Archers, and I'm proud.'

My fanaticism may have been forced underground, but it remained resilient, like the French Resistance. I take this as living proof that inside every cohabiting person there is a single person humming 'Dum de dum de dum de dum' waiting to get out.

The more I think about it, the more I impress myself – the clever ways I found to mask my addiction. I remember those Sunday mornings when I would grab the car-keys at around 10.13am, saying, 'Just popping down to Croydon for the Sunday papers, dear. I shouldn't be more than, oooh, let's say an hour.' And I would dash off and sit in the car with dark glasses on, agog to the omnibus edition on the car radio. I don't suppose the boyfriend ever suspected anything – although he did say: 'Why are you taking a flask of cocoa?' and 'What's wrong with buying them from the man on the corner?'

I expect the Archers euphoria stage was something Wittgenstein went through, too – and Edward Gibbon, I shouldn't wonder. The other novelties certainly wore off, in time. The tidying of newspapers, for example, started to look like a mug's game, so I ditched it. I expect I can call in a specialist with a fork-lift truck when I can't kick a path to the window any more.

For a while, too, I made a point of playing records with significant words – 'I'm Gonna Wash That Man Right Out of My Hair'; also 'I'm Still Standing' by Elton John – and lectured friends on the potency of cheap music.

But now the flat is sometimes eerily quiet, and I rattle around in it, like a lone Malteser in a shoebox. It is an odd thing, this single life. And Gloria Steinem's famous feminist axiom – that a woman without a man is like a fish without a bicycle – has been of strangely little comfort. I agree with the sentiment, but I wish she had chosen a different image. Unfortunately I find it very easy to imagine a sardine on a mountain-bike joyfully bowling along country lanes; or a tuna in a yellow jersey winning the Tour de France on the happiest day of its life.

One of the consolations of getting older is that one day you look in your address book and find you have acquired a list of specialists (hairdresser, mechanic, hypnotherapist, carpet-layer) whom you can mention in conversation and pass on to your friends. 'Try my Ear, Nose and Throat man,' you say, offhandedly. Or, 'My acupuncturist knows an aromatherapist who recommends a plumber who could really help you with that!' Gosh, it makes you feel sophisticated. And at the same time, of course, it helps you fill the rather big address book (with pussy-cats on) that somebody gave you for Christmas.

I now have a builder, a carpenter, a gas man, and a painter and decorator. Most exciting of all, however, is the handsome '24-hour emergency gardener', whose services I unfortunately rarely need. I sometimes think of him in the small hours, though, and picture him trouble-shooting in a dark garden somewhere, lashing daffs to splints in a high wind, looking Lawrentian. Should I call up with a bogus middle-of-the-night problem? 'Thank God you're there!' I might say, feigning a verge-of-tears voice. 'It's – er, a 24-hour emergency! And here I am, clothed only in these – er, diaphanous jim-jams, unequal to the struggle with the elements!'

The only glaring hole in my list of blokes is under 'window cleaner', because the local chap simply refuses to clean my windows, on the grounds (I think) that I didn't register with him in 1948. 'Excuse me,' I say periodically, pretending that the idea is quite a new one, and that we have never had the conversation before. 'You wouldn't do *my* windows, would you?' He looks down at me from his position on the ladder, and just says 'No', but he packs the word with an impressive degree of hostility and affront. My question seems to offend him; I don't know why. I mean, he *is* a window cleaner.

I mention all this because it is a great advantage of the single life to be able to say 'There is something wrong with the heating; I think I'll get a man in,' without having to negotiate with the boyfriend first. Boyfriends, I find, tend to reply 'No, let me take a look, I'm sure it's straightforward,' and end up emptying the S-bend on to their shoes at three in the morning. However competent the boyfriend, the sight of him with his head in the gas cupboard and the sound of bang!-clink!-Oops! is enough to make my blood run cold. 'What do you mean, Oops?' I say, dancing about in panic. 'Nothing.' 'You said Oops!' 'No I didn't.' 'You did.'

The trouble is that you start to identify with the boyfriend's tussle with his ego, which is getting out of hand. And strangely, no amount of hand-wringing or helpful why-don't-you-call-it-a-day noises make his tussle any easier. 'It's just this last hole,' he says grimly, after a day of constant drilling, and you peek aghast into a room filled with brick dust and a wall that has been drilled so many times it resembles pegboard. The helpful suggestion, 'Hey, let's forget those silly old shelves, and give the books to the Russians!' fails to lift the gloom.

Which is why I prefer the professional option. This is a simple business arrangement. If the bloke has problems with the job, his ego is his own affair. Recently, a rather lugubrious gas engineer came to remove the old pump from my central heating, and when he said 'Oh dear, oh dear, it won't budge an inch,' and 'Do you know, when you can get one side to come loose, the other side always sticks,' I just said 'Really?' and carried on watching daytime TV. Afterwards, when he discovered his car had been towed away from outside my house, I did not identify with his wounded pride. I drove him to the car pound and told him the fine was usually about eighty quid.

Left to my own resources, I admit I do sometimes 'get a man in' when it is not strictly necessary. I once called a heating engineer when the only problem was that I had turned the thermostat the wrong way; similarly I recently called out a bemused Zanussi man merely to clean the filter on my washing machine. A live-in partner might have stopped me, perhaps; but on the other hand, I might equally have come home to find bits of washing machine all over the floor, and a scribbled note 'Don't use water. Have gone to Zanussi spare parts centre in Cornwall,' while the culprit filter sat unnoticed, cocooned in soggy fluff.

On acquiring a boyfriend, then, it is important to know that a chap who says enthusiastically 'Why don't we knock the two rooms into one?' is not necessarily an expert with a sledge-hammer. He has just always fancied the idea of knocking down a wall. A friend of mine was married to a chap possessed of this spirit of enquiry, who carried a Swiss Army penknife at all times, and would offer to make new holes in watch-straps (sometimes when you didn't want one). At dinner parties he was noted for telling stories of fast-thinking chaps with Swiss Army penknives who had saved lives by performing emergency tracheotomies. Understandably, everybody kept quite quiet after this, and chewed very carefully. The slightest choke, and you knew he was likely to leap from his seat and cut your throat. To him, it was the ultimate Do It Yourself.

⌒

You want to meet Vic,' said Jonathan a few months ago, when I was having a therapeutic snivel one evening after a movie.

'Why?' I sobbed.

'Because he's a great bloke,' he said, heartily. 'Don't be so suspicious all the time, Lynne. Loosen up. Vic is a real free spirit, with marvellous ideas, and funnily enough his last girl-friend just threw him out so he's available. Some sort of bust-up over money, I think. Anyway, I'll introduce you.'

'What does he do?' I sniffed.

'He's very young at heart. Ha ha good old Vic.'

'What does he do, though?'

'Well, he's very artistic, and he's promised himself that if he doesn't get into something by the time he's forty-eight, he'll get a proper job.'

I thought about it. The distinct odour of rat whiffled past my nostrils, unignorably.

'Does he like cats?' I asked at last.

'No, he's allergic, I think.'

'Thank goodness for that, then,' I sighed with relief. 'I had an awful feeling for a moment that he was exactly my type.'

I hate to be the bearer of bad news, but Vic is a phenom-enon of our times. I used to think I was unlucky, but then I found out I was just single and averagely tolerant of failure, which made me a pushover for layabouts. It is possible that married readers are unfamiliar with the world of Vic, but each single woman discovers him for herself in a very short while. The telltale clue is when you find yourself paying for both dinners, but pretending not to notice. 'Did I? Never mind, it's only money. Tell me again about this project for knitting old cassette tape into lightweight blankets for the homeless, and charging them ten quid each. It sounds fascinating.'

Feminists, of course, are not supposed to admit that there is a man shortage. We have this horrible feeling that it will give ammunition to the backlash, who will jump up and down saying 'Tee hee! Told you! Only yourselves to blame!' But if there *were* a man shortage, hypothetically speaking, and it stretched out arid and flat to the far horizon, then you see that little shimmering dot in the distance? The one coming steadily towards you, like Omar Sharif in *Lawrence of Arabia*, getting slowly bigger and bigger and more sinister, as the only sign of available life? It's Vic.

'Tinker, tailor, soldier, sailor, Vic,' goes the prune-counting of the wised-up single woman each morning. 'Rich man, poor man, Vic, beggar man, thief, Vic.' Vic ought to be more substantially represented in this litany, really; but you get the gist. The really interesting thing, however, is not that single women are eating too many prunes. It is that Vic, like the devil, is everywhere, yet always comes as a surprise. When he's somebody else's Vic, you can identify him at once. Whereas when he is your own, and he is blatantly using your mains electricity to recharge his car battery again, you can't.

'Ooh, so when will I get to meet him?' you say to a friend who recently went out with Vic on a first date.

'Soon, I expect. He's moved in.'

There is a short pause, while you tell yourself it's none of your business.

'Really?' you say, non-committally.

'It's working out quite well, actually. I mean, being home all day he can take in the milk.'

'Great.'

'And he cooks meals and things, and above all he trusts me with his problems.'

'What does he do, then, exactly?'

'He's such a free spirit. Ha ha good old Vic.'

'No, but what does he do?'

'He used to be a disc jockey. And he's got so many schemes he doesn't know where to start. He reckons he needs a mobile phone and some headed notepaper before he can really get going. But unfortunately he hasn't got either at the moment.'

'He sounds – er, laid back.'

'Yes! Sometimes we laugh about it. I say he's so laid back he'll fall off and hurt himself.'

'Ho ho,' you say, politely.

They are not all called Vic, incidentally. It would make things too easy if they were. But I do feel it is worthwhile to list a few of the obvious warning signs, so that more women can be spared the misery of asking Vic, on some fateful day, 'Did you only love me for my free battery-charging facilities?' and then waiting for five agonizing minutes while he seriously weighs up the pros and cons. The term 'free spirit' ought to set alarm bells clanging; also Vic's habit of abruptly crossing the road to avoid walking past his bank. Watch out, too, for his suggestion (curious for a free spirit, after all) that you take out wills in one another's favour after only a brief acquaintance.

The really clever thing about Vic is that he feels most comfortable with women who are independent, for reasons beyond the obvious. To an independent woman, you see, the notion of sponging is so unthinkable that she can't bring herself to accuse anybody else of doing it. But the sad fact is, there are people in the world who consider themselves perfectly eligible for relationships yet whose personal motto is the same as New Hampshire's: 'Live Free or Die'. And unfortunately they don't all wear it on a T-shirt.

꿈

They will sack me when they read this. But how can I keep pretending to be single when I have recently entered a rather serious relationship? Ho hum, another nice job down the drain. Of course, I didn't mean to get into anything so heavy. In fact, I struggled quite hard against it.

'Don't you understand?' I moaned, sinking dramatically to my knees, and hammering my fist on the Axminster. 'I just can't afford to get into this. I mean, literally. I *can't afford* to get into this.'

It all started in June, when I took a few days' holiday at a hotel on the north Norfolk coast, all by myself. I had envisioned a carefree time, joining boat-trip excursions to blustery sand-spit nesting grounds, pedalling my nice bike down poppy-lined B roads, and enjoying solitary meals in the hotel dining room with just a book for company. For of course (ha ha) I thought of it as 'just a book', then.

'I'm taking *Possession*, by A.S. Byatt,' I breezily informed the cats while I packed (hoping they would be impressed). 'You know *Possession*, kitties: big one, really literary, Booker Prize-winner, everybody's read it already, bit of a mouthful so they say.' And I slung it in with the socks. None of us guessed what the future would hold – that after six warm days and nights of intimate contact with *Possession*, we would be locked in a tight stranglehold of book-and-woman relationship that would probably last for the rest of my literate life.

It is peculiar. I feel as though I have been married for forty years to the same book. *Possession* and I are not on the same wavelength, yet somehow I can't break free, and there is no literary equivalent to Relate.

Last week, when somebody asked me to a dinner party, I said automatically: 'Do you mind if I bring my book?' And they said, er, no, of course not.

But they didn't anticipate the change in me. We turned up at 7.30 (*Possession* and I) and sat quietly in a corner; and then we left together at about 10. 'Are you sure everything is all right?' whispered my host in the hall, as he showed us out. And I shrugged and raised my eyes to the ceiling, as if to say: 'What I have to put up with.'

I got in the car and put *Possession* on the passenger seat, and thought back to our early days at the hotel, where my fellow diners often drew attention to my book at meal times.

I had thought it was funny, then, the way their friendly comments would have sounded frankly presumptuous had I been seated with a bloke instead. How would a chap react, I wondered, if strangers kept leaning over him to say to me, 'Gosh, that's a big one,' and 'But I can't say I fancy it myself'?

Oh, what a Jezebel I used to be, when it came to books. 'Use 'em up and cast 'em aside' was my motto, as I notched up conquests on the bedpost, and blew smoke rings at the ceiling. I made bibliophile a dirty word. 'Use it gently, won't you?' people said when they lent me books, and I laughed, callously, with a succession of 'Heh!' noises. Living dangerously, I defied P.J. O'Rourke's prudent advice that you should always read stuff that will make you look good if you die in the middle of it. Let death surprise me in *flagrante* with the *Jeeves Omnibus*, I cared not.

And now here I am, stuck in terminal monogamy with *Possession*, a book I shall certainly die in the middle of, because I shall never finish it.

I keep reading the same bits over and over again, you see, because the story glances off my imagination without sticking. 'Try skim-reading,' my friends advise me, but I am not that kind of girl. I weep, I rage, I do the kneeling and hammering thing on the carpet. But the book remains calm and implacable on the coffee table, its nice blue ribbon marking my place. I complain about *Possession* to my mum on the phone ('We just don't get on, mum'), and she says loyally: 'Why don't you bust up, like you did with old whatsisname, Henry James, that time?'

Sometimes, when you are unhappy in a relationship, it is good to talk about it. But it breaks your heart to think how casually it was undertaken in the first place. I mean, I only thought, 'Better not take a funny book' (since it sometimes disturbs people's dinners when you suddenly bark explosively, sending bits of half-digested bread roll across the room); and

'I won't take any Anita Brookner, especially not the ones about lonely old maids reading in restaurants.'

Of such chance decisions are our manacles forged.

It is no good regretting it now. It is no good thinking of Dorothy Parker's famous line, 'This is not a novel to be tossed aside lightly, it should be thrown with great force.' I sit glumly in my living room, humming the tune to 'A Fine Romance' in a minor key, and guiltily running my eyes over the books pages of newspapers while pretending not to.

Possession does not satisfy me: it is as simple as that. And all I can do is pace outside Waterstone's on wet afternoons, feverishly wondering whether I dare run in, grab a copy of *Madame Bovary* and take it on an illicit ride in a cab.

News Stories That Captured
My Imagination

I would like you to imagine the following narrative and see what is wrong with it. A woman, in Virginia, drives at top speed away from the house where she has just severed her husband's penis. She is by nature a long-suffering person (as evidenced by her placid acceptance of her married name – Bobbitt – with all its connotations of finger puppets), but under the strain of the relationship she has finally snapped like a dry stick, and now she hares away from the grisly scene. She tosses the offending pizzle from the car window and drives on. All this may sound implausible, but in credibility terms it is easy meat compared with the next bit. For, shortly after, the police arrive, locate the member, pack it in ice and nee-naw it to a hospital (doubtless singing encouraging songs to it, to keep its peck – I mean, er, to boost its morale), where it is successfully re-attached to a grateful Mr Bobbitt.

Now my point is this. If you leave a trowel in the long grass next to the shed, you can't find it, can you? If you drop a clothes-peg on the kitchen floor and it bounces sideways, it can disappear for weeks. Yet for some reason Mr Bobbitt's severed member was found easily by the side of a busy road. Is this not suspicious? If I were Mr Bobbitt, what would really worry me right now is not the imminent outcome of the court case against Mrs Bobbitt, nor even the off-colour willy-jokes at my expense ('It will never stand up in court,' and so on). No, I would be thinking: do I have the right willy? What if those well-meaning state troopers, scouring the dusty roadside ('There it is! We got it!'), actually located somebody else's?

You may not remember the old German film *The Hands of Orlac*, but it is relevant, I promise. The plot concerned a virtuoso pianist who by a crushing misfortune loses both his hands in a railway accident, but whose career is ostensibly saved when a scientist secretly sews on some donor hands belonging to a freshly hanged murderer, whose dexterous speciality happened to be strangling and knife-throwing. Doubtless you can see where this is leading. The post-operative pianist peers at his big mitts ('They don't look like mine,' he comments, but tragically lets it pass), and then tries to practise some scales, only to find that – musically speaking – his new fingers have 'Geest' and 'Fyffes' written all over them. It is peculiar. Then one day his fiancée's newspaper is snatched by a gust of wind, and he automatically picks up a Sabatier, yells 'Leave this to me!', and hurls the knife with such deadly accuracy that it nails the paper to the floor. Naturally, there is a significant pause while she looks at him, and he looks at the knife, and then they both look at his sewn-on hands, with glum expressions.

Reports of Mr Bobbitt's operation tell us it was only partially successful. In other words, *it is not the willy that it used to be*. Enough said, I think. Much attention Stateside has focused on the advisability of women taking the law into their own hands, and on the disturbing idea that here, in the Bobbitt emasculation, is the most terrifying of all female revenges. But of course it isn't, not by a long measure. A proper job would involve detailed pre-planning, and in particular the planting of a look-alike willy on a main road (a stand-in!), possibly next to a large sign with 'I think this is what you're looking for, officer' written in large letters upon it. In the sweetest of all possible revenges, Mr Bobbitt would therefore emerge from his anaesthetic and say, 'Funny, doesn't look like mine,' but cast such doubt immediately from his thoughts, as impossibly far-fetched.

Tattooed serial numbers would seem to be the answer, if any man is worried. But I doubt Mrs Bobbitt with her kitchen knife has started a trend, or anything. Most women are rightly repulsed by the idea of mutilation; if there is a nasty cackle of joy among certain feminists at the Bobbitt news, it's just that there is something irresistibly hilarious at the idea of standing between a man and his willy, for however brief a span. I just hope the Hollywood Bobbitt films have thought of the *Orlac* angle. It would be a shame not to grab it up, rush it to the studios, and stitch it on sharpish. After all, it wouldn't even matter if it didn't quite fit.

'Bob Dylan has been spotted looking at property in Crouch End ...'
Scene: The well-furnished drawing-room of a large house in Crouch End, north London, one afternoon in August. Birds twitter in the garden beyond; a doorbell rings; a dog barks. From the hallway, a small shriek of surprise is followed by low murmurings of welcome. The door to the drawing-room opens briefly and an estate agent is heard to say, 'Upstairs first, I think,' before a woman, evidently distraught, rushes in, slams the door and grabs the telephone. She dials and waits, screwing up her face and tap-dancing on the parquet in anguish and impatience. Finally her call is answered by a man with a German accent.

WOMAN: Doctor Fiegelman? Thank God you're there. It's happening again.

DR FIEGELMAN (*on phone*): Go on.

WOMAN (*with strangled cry*): It's Bob Dylan, doctor. He wants to buy the house.

DR F: *Mein Gott*, this is serious. Are you sitting down?

WOMAN: No.

DR F: I think you should sit down.

The woman miserably slides down the wall until she is sitting on the floor.

WOMAN (*whispering*): Done it.

DR F: Good. Now, taking your time, what exactly is it that makes you think Bob Dylan wants to buy your house in Crouch End?

WOMAN: The fact that he is currently upstairs with an estate agent investigating the airing cupboard!

DR F: I see. And when did this start?

WOMAN: The minute I opened the door.

DR F: Mm.

WOMAN: You've got to help me, doctor.

DR F: And I shall. But I thought we finished with all this after Al Pacino bought that old cooker-hood you advertised in *Loot*?

WOMAN (*faintly*): So did I.

DR F: I mean, Elizabeth Taylor never turned up for the hairdrier, did she?

WOMAN: No. Not after we worked on it for two months, five days a week, at £75 a go.

DR F: And you realized, in the end, that it wasn't Warren Beatty who bought the pram?

WOMAN: It was – um, David Essex?

DR F: That's right. Not Warren Beatty, but David Essex. That's very good. You've been doing the breathing exercises?

WOMAN: Every day.

DR F: And how big is this Bob Dylan?

WOMAN: Quite small.

DR F: Thank God for that, at any rate.

Suddenly the door opens, and BOB DYLAN *enters the room, carrying a tape-measure and wearing a puzzled expression. The* WOMAN *whispers hoarsely into the phone, 'I'll call you back,' and hangs up. She scrambles to her feet, looking guilty.*

WOMAN (*nervously*): Ha ha.

DYLAN smiles politely, strolls to the french window, looks at the view, shrugs, mumbles something appreciative, and exits. The WOMAN points wordlessly at his departing back, and then faints on the hearth-rug. Black-out, curtain.

Scene: The same, an hour later. MAN with briefcase, evidently returning from work, enters to find wife lying insensate on the best Persian. Thinking quickly, he hurls his briefcase at her recumbent form, and it bounces off her head.

MAN: Darling, speak to me!

WOMAN (rubbing her bonce, indicating the briefcase): Why did you do that?

MAN: I didn't have a glass of water.

WOMAN: I see.

MAN: Why are you on the carpet? Not another of your delusions, poppet?

The WOMAN nods, reluctantly.

MAN (sympathetically): Not Michael Jackson offering to spay the cat again?

WOMAN: No. Bob Dylan, wanting to buy the house, for £310,000.

The MAN whistles through his teeth.

MAN: £310,000? Well that's something. Good heavens, £310,000, it might almost cover the therapy. I mean, what did we get for the cooker-hood?

WOMAN: Five pounds. But –

MAN: I think we should go for it.

The doorbell rings. The MAN prepares to answer it. He re-enters, dumbfounded, with ELIZABETH TAYLOR at his side.

MISS TAYLOR (for it is she): Sorry I'm late, I've come to collect the hairdrier.

As the curtain falls, the WOMAN collapses into her husband's arms, and ROBERT DE NIRO enters whistling with a bucket and ladder, asking to use the tap. End.

The front-page headline of last Thursday's *East London Advertiser* was rather alarming, especially for the sort of neurotic pet-owner who periodically grabs her cat by the shoulders and searches its furry, inscrutable face, saying with a choked voice, 'You've got to tell me something. If I died, would you eat me?'

'DEAD MAN "EATEN" IN GRUESOME CAT HORROR' screamed the headline, thereby putting an end to all speculation. Of course I hoped it was a sensational joke – along the lines of the *Weekly World News*: 'Bat With Human Face Found (He's Smart As A Whip, Says Expert)' – but I knew in my heart it was serious. Evidently, this poor chap in Shadwell died of a heart attack, and in the ensuing week his thirty cats – starving hungry, but with no money for Whiskas, and anyway congenitally hopeless with a tin-opener – perpetrated the gruesome cat horror which involved him being 'eaten'. It doesn't bear thinking about. Apparently he loved those cats. He thought they loved him back. So far as I could see, the only positive aspect to the story was that he was 'eaten' only in inverted commas.

I don't usually see the *East London Advertiser*, but a kind friend sent me the cutting, thinking I ought to know. Possibly she recalled that my latest effort to tighten the bond with my own cats entails entertaining them each morning with spirited impersonations of the animals they are about to eat, which suddenly smacks of insane recklessness, given the Shadwell experience. 'Now, what have we got here?' I say excitedly, examining the tin. They give me a weary ironical look that says, 'Go on, surprise us.' 'Rabbit!' I raise the tin-opener, and their ears prick up, so I put it down again and they scan the ceiling for flies. 'A rabbit goes like this,' I say, assuming the goofy-teeth thing, and waggling my hands on top of my head, in semblance of floppy ears. They look at each other in despair. 'How's she going to do liver, that's what I'd like to know?'

(Incidentally, sorry to interrupt the flow, but for anyone thinking of adopting this pleasurable and essentially harmless daily routine, here are some tips. First, it is hard to imitate salmon unless you have a fairly high ceiling, for the leaping upstream. Kidneys and liver are indeed virtually impossible to impersonate, and should therefore be eliminated at the shopping-trolley stage. For high-class meals involving crab, one needs an energetic sideways scuttle, so clear all furniture first. The turkey impression comes to life splendidly if you can be bothered to tie empty red balloons to the sides of your head. Beef, lamb and duck are a doddle, obviously. And finally, a word of warning: if you find yourself trying to impersonate a chunk *per se*, you may have let things get out of hand.)

Anyway, in my initial alarm at this story, I kept thinking of that famous scene in Charlie Chaplin: the snow-bound cabin, the two companions ravenous, and the fat man with the heavy eye-liner hallucinating that the little fellow is a chicken. How ghastly to think this is happening in my own home – and not just when I am selflessly attempting to enliven mealtimes with a spot of one-sided Old MacDonald charades. When they watch me trotting to the shed, those cats just see a huge tin of Whiskas on legs. When I'm asleep, they see a huge tin of Whiskas, with legs, lying on its side.

But the interesting thing about the Shadwell story was the line, 'The RSPCA had been called in, to destroy the cats.' What? Destroyed? Why on earth would you do that? Suddenly all my sympathies swung the other way. These cats should be counselled for post-traumatic stress. It is a well-observed fact that in *extremis* human beings will cannibalize each other; and we don't generally hand the bewildered survivors to a humane vet afterwards. These cats needed food, there was nothing depraved about it. Imagine you were locked in a Kellogg's warehouse, and helped yourself to a few Rice Krispies to keep yourself alive. At the end of the week, the police burst in, and you say, 'Thank God you've come, there's not a drop of milk in this place, can you believe that?' But they survey the scene – snap, crackle and pop all over the place – and shrink back, screaming. 'CEREALS "EATEN" IN GRUESOME VEGETARIAN HORROR' runs the headline in next week's paper, and you are peremptorily taken out and shot.

The Single Woman Considers Going Out but Doesn't Fancy the Hassle

I have been toying with an idea for a short story. It's a variation on the film *Thelma and Louise*, in which a third, previously overlooked woman character (let's call her Abigail) gets a phone call from Louise. 'Git yer bags, honey, me and Thelma we're headin' fer the mountens.' 'Count me in,' yells the feisty Abigail as the soundtrack swells with up-beat jive. She paints her lips, grabs a sweater, pulls on her cowgirl boots, swings through the door and then stops on the porch. Damn. The music ceases abruptly. She puts down her bag and kicks it. Damn again. What has she been thinking of? How can she go? How can she possibly go on a once-in-a-lifetime adventure with Louise and Thelma today – *when she's already started defrosting a chicken?*

I intend to call the story 'The Road More Travelled', because I feel the majority of women will identify with Abigail the chicken lady. My sorrowful contention, in fact, is that butter it how you will, we are most of us chicken ladies – rationalizing inaction, inventing pathetic reasons not to do things. Why didn't the chicken lady cross the road? Because she'd just done her toenails, of course. For every Thelma and Louise accelerating a big green Thunderbird into thin air above the Grand Canyon there are at least a million of us pressing our noses to wet wintry windscreens, deciding we can't possibly take a five-minute detour on the way back from Ikea. 'Got to get home!' Why? 'It's bins night.'

The trouble with escape, I suppose, is that it must be dramatic and once-and-for-all; anything else is just holidays. For my own part, I have nothing particularly onerous at home to escape from – only newspaper deadlines, a neglected novel, an *EastEnders* addiction, and a punishing schedule of cats' tea-times – yet I seem to battle constantly against powerful flight fantasies. I don't mean drooling over economy fares to Delhi, either. I mean that regularly I drive in circles at Brighton's orbital roundabouts, defying the lure of the home exit, and torturing myself with such exotic alternatives as 'Worthing' and 'Shoreham'.

Yes, yes, make the break! Turn those wheels, baby! But then I glance at the clock on the dashboard and change my mind. Drat, half-past two, it will be dark in a couple of hours. If you're going to run away from home, it's better to hit the road first thing in the morning with a little bag of Marmite sandwiches and a banana. So I take the Brighton turn-off with a familiar mixture of self-loathing and relief, and head back by the usual route. (*Today's unconvincing reason for not escaping: no banana.*)

I hope I'm not talking to myself here, by the way. Perhaps some readers never entertain the 'Ordinary Woman Completely Disappears' fantasy; never dream of wearing dark glasses at night and crashing through road-blocks on the A27 at Chichester. But surely every woman turns down small adventures in favour of urgent ironing; says 'Can't' when she really means something else. Perhaps we draw the line so quickly on outlandish opportunities because we fear otherwise it may not get drawn at all. Thelma and Louise discover what they're capable of once they're free, and it's pretty alarming.

But back at my short story, I don't know how it ends. I don't know what happens to Abigail the chicken lady. In the movie, when Thelma and Louise drive at night through Monument Valley, you get that spooky old Marianne Faithfull song 'The Eyes of Lucy Jordan' about the woman who went bonkers because she always stayed home. 'At the age of 37 / She realized she'd never / Drive through Paris in a sports car / With the warm wind in her hair.' I have an idea that Abigail has no such regrets. She just continues to defrost the chicken, cooks it, suffers salmonella poisoning and dies – expiring just at the point when Thelma and Louise fly into their ravine. It's a bit harsh, perhaps. But as *Thelma and Louise* showed, sometimes you have to be fairly dramatic to make a point.

In the new *Penguin Book of British Comic Writing* there is a short autobiographical essay by Elizabeth Bowen called 'On Not Rising to the Occasion'. I recommend it highly, especially if your memory of childhood etiquette disasters is still so vivid it makes you feel like running to the hall and burying your face in an auntie's funny-smelling coat. Elizabeth Bowen's childhood was an Edwardian one, so she had proper guidance in suitable behaviour (she probably did not innocently repeat the word 'git' in company, as I did), but she still misjudged it sometimes in a very particular way: she 'overshot the mark'. 'Thank you, Mrs Robinson, so very, very much for the absolutely wonderful LOVELY party!' she would say. 'Well, dear,' her hostess would reply with a frigid smile, 'I'm afraid it was hardly so wonderful as all that.'

My own experience of childhood parties was a little different, since I felt awkward in the society of children and generally slipped out during pass-the-parcel to ask Mrs Robinson whether I could help with the washing up – which surprised her, especially if we hadn't eaten yet. 'No, you go and have a good time,' she said, mystified, pushing me out of the kitchen with her leg. Thus, when it came to going-home time, I did not embarrass her with my effusions; I merely cried with relief. 'Lynne tried to help with the washing up,' she would inform my older sister, tapping her forehead significantly. 'Funny,' said my sister. 'She doesn't do that at home.'

But I still managed to overshoot the mark in other ways. At the age of ten, for example, I went to a party where a game of forfeits was played – you know, where you are given a task, and the penalty for failure is to kiss a boy. When my turn came (and I had been led back to the games room by a kind but firm Mrs Robinson, who declined my wild-eyed offer of silver-polishing) I was informed that my task was to recite a poem. A limerick would have easily sufficed. But I was nervous, and desperate not to kiss a boy, so I launched into 'The Highway-man', a long, galloping poem which unfortunately galloped off with me clinging on to its back, bouncing and helpless. In fact, I had got as far as 'Tlot-tlot in the frosty silence!' before the exasperated kids finally flung themselves bodily in front of my runaway poem, waving their arms, to make me stop.

Overshooting the mark in Elizabeth Bowen's sense is actually quite difficult these days, now that we have followed America into a more kissy-huggy way of life. Saying merely 'Thank you for the absolutely wonderful LOVELY party!' sounds tame, actually; it raises suspicions that you didn't enjoy it. In 1978, when Woody Allen's film *Interiors* came out, I remember that it seemed genuinely peculiar to see women greet each other with 'Hey! You look great! Your green is perfect!' while planting smackeroos on one another's ear-rings. Nobody I knew behaved like that. But now I don't know anybody who doesn't. In fact nowadays, if someone neglects to applaud my green, I actually worry about it afterwards.

But what Elizabeth Bowen's essay brought to my mind most horribly was not the thank-you-for-having-me thing; or even the social smackeroo. What it made me think of most was Selfridges. Because one day, when I was in the basement there, I quite unwittingly overshot the mark, and I still feel embarrassed about it. It happened quite by chance; I had only popped in for some *diamanté* cat collars. But then I noticed this poor old bloke on a carpet-tiled plinth demonstrating a cordless travel iron, and I'm afraid it was 'The Highwayman' all over again.

The trouble was, his little crowd was so unresponsive. 'Now, you see this?' he said, without much enthusiasm, producing a bone-dry knotted lump of cotton velvet. Nobody moved, or indeed acknowledged his presence, so I piped up, I couldn't help it. 'Gosh,' I chuckled encouragingly, 'I wouldn't want to iron *that*!' He gave me a look, then gravely un-knotted the velvet and flourished his little iron over it – to amazing effect. Suddenly the cloth was smooth and lovely! Again, nobody clapped, or even murmured. So I said quite loudly, 'Well, I think that's quite remarkable. I've never seen anything like it. What an extraordinary device. I only came in for these cat collars and a whole new world has been revealed.'

And I got increasingly voluble, I don't know why. 'That's amazing,' I said flatly, as his crowd started to wander off. 'Do that again. Wow, I can't believe how those creases are coming out.' I felt I was doing him a useful turn, although I couldn't help noticing that by the time the demonstration ended I was the only person left. 'Thank you,' I said warmly, 'that was marvellous,' and went off to pay for the cat collars. And when I looked back, I noticed he was pointing me out to a sales assistant, who was patting him gently on the shoulder.

Only when I got home did I realize I had overshot the mark so badly I had sounded like a 'plant', by which time it was too late to apologize. I often wonder how close I got, actually, to being clocked over the bonce with a miracle travel iron. It would have been such a pointless way to go. Whatever the merits of this extraordinary velvet-smoother, it was hardly so wonderful as all that.

⌒

One of the more obvious advantages of childlessness is that you never have to do the business with the school hamster. We all know the syndrome: it starts with 'Can we have Raffles at home this weekend?' and ends when after forty-eight hours of love and attention – feeding, watering and changing straw – the motley, beady-eyed ingrate suddenly kicks the bucket on Sunday night when all the pet shops are shut. Stiff-legged on the floor of his hutch, the hamster peers through its straw with a great eternal question in its lifeless gaze. It appears to be thinking, 'Get out of that. You can't, can you?'

But unfortunately single life does bring its own version of the Death of Raffles routine. Since you tend not to take holidays at peak times (such as the first week in August), you can find yourself cheerfully agreeing to be pet-servicer, plant-waterer and fish-food-sprinkler for such a large number of lucky neighbouring holiday-makers that you would certainly bend under the burden of responsibility if the weight of all the flipping door-keys didn't stagger you first. Currently my key-ring is so heavy with other people's Chubbs, Banhams and Ingersolls that I am permanently reminded of the great clanking whatsit dragged around by Marley's Ghost.

I am quite happy to do it; besides, they do the same for me. I am just terrified that something will die, like Raffles, and break somebody's heart. Take the Herbs. For the past fortnight I have tended some little potted herbs, which evidently blossomed and thrived until I came along, but have subsequently withered on the stalk, and are now succumbing in heaps, like a herbaceous equivalent of the last act of *Hamlet*. Each time I pop my head around the door, a basil plant whispers 'I die' or 'The rest is silence' and collapses; it is ghastly. To my returning friend it will look as though Agent Orange has swept through her kitchen on a pale horse. Twice a day I creep in, ostensibly to do more hopeful watering, but mainly to confront the horror and measure the devastation. I shall never be able to look a plate of pesto in the face again.

Latch-key duty is one of those rare things in life (operating the red button in a nuclear silo is another) where the sense of onerous responsibility is out of all proportion to the teensy effort required. Perhaps that's why it worries me so much. Feeding fish takes precisely fifteen seconds, but the fear of forgetting such a tiny thing gives me sleepless nights.

Also, I feel awkward letting myself in to someone's house: I don't look around, I don't breathe, and the sound of my own voice ('Hello fishies, ha ha, still alive?') gives me the creeps. The whole operation being so brief and automatic, I assume at midnight I must have got it all mixed up. Perhaps I sprinkled fish-food on the curtains. Perhaps I watered the cat.

Of course, some people must do it differently. Keys give them the run of the place, and they love it. They let themselves in, light a cigarette, put the kettle on, and start rummaging in your sock-drawer for interesting ticket-stubs, so that they can startle you a week later by asking 'How was *Night of the Iguana*, by the way?' Obviously this is the sort of fish-food-sprinkler to avoid, but sometimes you don't recognize them until it is too late. Once, a friend of mine asked a chronically inquisitive chap actually to reside in her flat for a week while she took a holiday; and rashly ignored the warning signals when, immediately on hand-over, he whipped open cupboards and drawers in the manner of a professional burglar, saying, 'Anywhere you don't want me to look?' and 'Oh how very interesting. Fond of pink.'

Pretty loud warning signals, really; but she was late for a plane, so took a quick mental inventory of sexually incriminating material and decided to risk it. On holiday (with me), she fantasized (with my help) that her house-sitter was currently waltzing around the living-room dressed in her most expensive evening-frock, boozing direct from the bottle and leafing through her teenage diaries. She never discovered whether this alarming picture had any basis in reality, but when she asked him 'How was your stay?' he replied, 'Well, it did fill a few gaps.'

Having just popped out to see the herbs again, I can announce that a variegated sage has now turned peaky ('The drink, the drink – I am poisoned'), and my sense of failure is complete. It occurs to me belatedly that the friend who cat-sits for me when I go on holiday makes a point of spending 'quality time' with my cats, watching their favourite snooker videos with them and shouting at *The Archers* in a plucky imitation of me. I should do something similar with the herbs. After all, I know that my friend listens to Radio 3 and reads the *Independent*. An hour each day in their company, then, with the wireless blaring, and with me pretending to read her newspaper (exclaiming 'Swipe me, how pompous' in an authentic *Indie*-reader kind of way) might set them on the road to recovery.

Meanwhile I have started to wear my keys on a girdle, in the fashion of a Victorian housekeeper, shifting it from side to side on alternate days, to prevent curvature of the spine. I have always associated keys with the getting of wisdom, but since unlocking things seems to scare me so much (I lock them up again as quickly as possible) perhaps I should stick to the road of excess, instead. It is not much of an insight to boast of, in the end: that acting bored by the *Independent* might save the life of a flat-leaf parsley.

Having never given a second thought to the practice of diving into cinemas on the merest whim and spending two and a half hours in blissful solitary communion with a large screen and a sack of Opal Fruits, I was rather alarmed to discover recently that some of my friends think this marks me out as a desperate case.

'I went to see *The Fisher King* on Wednesday,' I announce cheerfully. 'On your own?' 'Er, yes.' 'Oh dear,' they say, and catch up my hand for a bout of sympathetic patting and smoothing. 'I ate two boxes of Fruit Pastilles,' I add hurriedly. 'Boy, you should have seen my tongue afterwards!' But they continue to shake their heads, with tears in their eyes. They think it is awful.

There is a stigma attached to it, you see; an atavistic idea that a woman sitting alone in a cinema is a woman self-evidently abandoned to the black dog of depression, and therefore a proper cause for public concern. Does this attitude reflect a rather deep, dark prejudice against the idea of women enjoying their own company? It is possible.

The real point is that I never, in any case, feel sorry for myself in a cinema. If you want to feel miserable, there are many more surefire ways of achieving it, after all: sit in a doorway with a homeless person; lean over a parapet on Waterloo Bridge and gaze into the mesmerically choppy waters; go and see how long *Starlight Express* has been running. The impulse simply to buy a ticket and sit comfortably in a dark public place of entertainment seems by comparison a whoop of life-affirming joy.

What I like is the feeling of sanctuary. Hugging my possessions to my chest, sinking low in the seat, and prising great juicy wads of Opal Fruit away from my molars, I feel tremendously comforted by the reflection that I have vanished off the face of the earth; nobody has a clue where I am. The phone won't ring; motorcycle messengers cannot pursue me. If it didn't cost £6.50, it would be like stepping through the wardrobe into Narnia. As I huddle down, and prepare to sneer at the now excruciatingly familiar advertisements, I like to imagine that my friends are all ringing each other in panic. 'She's gone to earth again.' 'Damn.' 'Now there's nothing we can do but wait.'

In old movie thrillers, of course, outlaws on the run frequently took refuge in cinemas. They would stoop as though entering church, shiftily taking aisle seats and removing their hats. They pretended to watch the picture, but kept a constant eye on the door, waiting for the inevitable pair of mackintoshed cops to appear, asking questions of the usherette. For them, the cinema was only a temporary haven; for me, it is total. While I may sometimes *feel* like a criminal, for instance, I have never yet been obliged to shoot my way out of an emergency exit after watching half a reel of the film.

But what is the alternative, anyway, to going alone? It is *to go with other people* – and are you telling me this is preferable? How many times has one agreed, casually, 'Hey, let's do a movie!' only to discover that one's good friend Mike has never been properly cinema-trained? Me, I like to concentrate on the film; but for the universal Mike the cinema is a place where people are mysteriously quiet and sober-sided, where they have forgotten the value of voluble free-association, and need to be reminded of it. He is a restless kind of guy, and chatty. I mean, is this a funeral, or what?

'Doesn't that bloke remind you of Phil?' he will chuckle loudly, briefly standing up to point at Mickey Rourke. I ignore him, of course, and bite my scarf, hoping that my explicitly hostile body language will tell him to shut up. It doesn't. 'Remind me to tell you later what Phil said at lunch-time,' he adds, with an exaggerated nudge to the ribs. 'It was such a scream.' He then performs a nonchalant spot of overhead juggling, using a Malteser, a carton of Kia-Ora and a fully extended umbrella.

On really bad days, moreover, it transpires that Mike also suffers strange lapses of concentration, rendering him incapable of following plot. 'What happened to the blonde girl?' he suddenly enquires, at a moment of maximum plot interest. 'Lynne, what happened to the blonde girl?' he repeats a little more loudly, thinking I haven't heard. 'She died,' I whisper back through clenched teeth. 'Really? When?' he asks. At which point I start to look round for the manager.

I suppose the tragic image of the single person in the cinema derives from the idea that they can't have any friends. Perhaps it is time for this assumption to be overturned – since it is more likely, in my opinion, that the lone cinema-goer is simply attempting to preserve the few friendships she has still got left. Personally I associate the plush seat and the bag of chews with nothing other than pleasure and freedom. For me, the really tragic aspect of cinema-going is to hear people say, 'Oh yes, I wanted to see JFK , but unfortunately I couldn't persuade anyone to come with me.' That's so *sad*.

⌒

I have started getting a bit peculiar in Sainsbury's. I knew it would happen eventually – that I would stop being Little Miss Reasonable at the check-out, and start getting verbal. 'There's no *point*, you know,' I say, waving my hand in the face of the woman on the till. 'There's no *point* checking these things through so fast, because I can't possibly pack them at the same rate.' She nods, but takes no notice; just sets her jaw and carries on rolling tins down the conveyor belt three times a second, in a manner reminiscent of a thousand infernal-machine scenes from Jerry Lewis and Jacques Tati movies.

I always buy the same things in supermarkets: multiple tins of cat-food, multiple pots of hummus, multiple rolls of swing-bin liners. Take my advice: if you are the teensiest bit neurotic

– can't cope with all the choices in the modern world, check all the taps twelve times before answering the phone, won't speak at dinner-parties until someone has said the word 'badger' – then shopping feels much less dangerous if you don't give any consideration to what you actually want to buy.

Cat-food, hummus, bin-liners; cat-food, hummus, bin-liners. I exercise an astounding degree of self-control in this respect, though on every trip I also give myself seven minutes for open-mouthed wonder, as I stand in front of the biscuit displays, eyes all aglow, and look at the lovely, lovely things that can be made by simply rubbing together fat, sugar and flour. When my seven minutes are over, I ritually push my trolley past temptation, and have a little sob by the free-range eggs.

The reason I'm going into all this is that I recently had a bit of a shock in the bin-liner department. There I was, feeling safe inside my routine, repeating to myself, 'Cat-food – yes; hummus – yes; bin-liners ...' and scooping an armful of boxes into my trolley, when I noticed a little yellow 'flash' had appeared on the side of the box. 'NEW,' it said: 'MULTI-PURPOSE.' In my confusion I dropped the lot. Staggering slightly, I reached out for support, and knocked some roasting-bags and double-length cling-film onto the floor as well. I tried to calm down by humming *Lillibullero* and sucking a tranquillizer, but it did no good. Should I climb up on top of the fitment and signal for assistance? What did it mean, 'Multi-Purpose'? What possible other purpose can there be for a bin-liner than to line bins? Had Sainsbury's brought out a 'Josceline Dimbleby Book of Bin-Liner Cookery'?

I don't like it; I don't like it at all. I always thought I knew where I was, knew what I was getting. Of course, I have *used* some of these so-called multi-purpose bin-liners. And of course they work just as well as the old Uni-Purpose kind ever did. But a sense of certainty has been lost now, that can never be restored. I daren't go back, not now. What if they've printed 'Not for external use' on the hummus, or 'Non-drip' on the Whiskas?

It's official. It was in the paper on Saturday. The reason women make good spooks (or employees of the secret service) is that they can deflect awkward personal questions, especially over dinner. 'So what do you do?' they are asked, routinely. And instead of excitedly blurting out the latest list of arms-deal catastrophes, they cleverly feign a suppressed yawn and say, 'Me? Oh, nothing. I have a boring desk job at the Ministry of Defence. Paperclips, that kind of thing. Dust, Turkish carpet, Cup-a-Soups, nine to five, calligraphy, tea-trolley, cheese rolls, Argos catalogue, Club biscuits.' These MI5 women are masterly at it, obviously. I imagine them left out of the general conversation, eating, listening. And whenever the talk threatens to veer back in their direction, they just mutter 'paperclips' again, and it's gone.

Men, on the other hand, tend to give the game away. Asked the same question, a man will evidently suck his teeth thoughtfully, smile into the middle distance, and then hoarsely whisper, 'Ooh, sorry, I'd love to, but classified, careless talk, Brixton, Circus, say no more' – at which everyone promptly stops talking or eating, and someone drops a fork. In the ensuing silence, he pretends to change the subject. 'Did you say you'd been to Prague for a holiday? Funny, I was once shot in the leg in Pr—.' He stops, looks around. 'Whoops, ha ha,' he jokes, 'No, but really let's talk about you and your allotment, I'm sure it's *much more interesting*.'

On Saturday, when this intriguing gender fact was first revealed, I have to admit I was confused. I always thought it was the other way around – that women talked openly (in my own case, compulsively) about their jobs, and that men did not. Well-mannered men, in particular, often refuse so obstinately to divulge their occupations – either they consider it impolite to boast, or they think you should know without asking – that you can sit next to a chap for hours, wildly demonstrating the special effects in *Jurassic Park* (complete with roars, thumps, tussles and realistic squirts of ketchup), before finally discovering that he's controller of Radio 3, or married to the Princess Royal. Sometimes you don't find out until it's too late to apologize. 'That was the Primate of All England,' someone will say to you at a party, nodding at your new friend as he wanders off, scratching his head. Numbly, you sink to the floor with your fingers in your mouth. You just asked him to take you dancing.

But what impresses me most is the thought of those high-powered women heroically pretending they wear slippers in the office. How do they cope with the follow-up questions? Or is it really true that if you say the words 'boring desk job', people will enquire no further?

I remember an alarming moment from an innocent girls' night out in Twickenham, when I came out of the Ladies to rejoin the little group of rugby fans we'd met (what larks!), and bumped into my friend, menacingly lying in wait. 'Stop saying you're a journalist,' she hissed, with the veins curiously sticking out on her neck. 'Why?' I said, jumping backwards. 'Because it scares off the blokes. Tell them you've got a boring desk job.' I was stunned. 'I can't,' I said. 'What if they ask a supplementary question?' She glared. She fumed. She danced on the spot. 'And trust you to use the word *supplementary*!' she barked, before barging through the swing door with a mighty shove from the shoulder.

I realize I could never be a spook. Not just because I would betray secret operations by careless dinner-party chat, but because I consider the invention of alter egos a dangerous practice. Surely it's hard enough being one person, without deliberately trying to be two. In order to keep saying 'boring desk job, oh yes, boring desk job', you would have to believe in it so completely – the Tube journey, the green triplicate forms – that surely one morning you would wake up and find it true, like something blackly paranoid out of Kafka, even down to the Club biscuits. The horror! 'Help me, someone, I worked for MI5 , and now I have a boring desk job!' you would yell, but no one would listen. 'But you *always* had a boring desk job,' they would say, with narrowed eyes, like conspirators. 'Or that's what you always *said*.'

The demise of the Protein Man of Oxford Street last week, at the age of seventy-eight, came as a bit of a shock. Not that I knew him, of course; it's just that in common with millions of Londoners I felt I had a vague idea what he had on his mind – mainly because it was written on a placard in big white letters immediately above his head. I apologize if you don't remember him.

How one hates, in a national newspaper, to strike the pose of the metropolitan bore (which reminds me, aren't they *rude* in Groucho's?); yet the ever-present solitary figure in the jostling shopping crowd with his flat cap and specs, his placard, and his deeply peculiar message – LESS PASSION FROM LESS PROTEIN – so far resembles a universal archetype that, as a Londoner, I can hardly believe Stanley Owen-Green just wore a groove in the dusty pavements of Oxford Street for twenty-five years, with outings to Putney Bridge for the Boat Race. Perhaps it helps to say that, like Zelig in the Woody Allen film, the Protein Man was present in every black-and-white picture of London crowds that one has ever seen.

The point about Mr Green was that he was against protein.

I emphasize this because although he devoted the last third of his life to carrying a placard above his head, and possibly sleeping in an extra-long bed to accommodate it at nights, he did not make it easy for the average foreign shopper, stooped under the weight of cheesy meaty nutty food purchases from Selfridges, to understand immediately what he meant.

At the same time as spreading dietary awareness Mr Green also engendered considerable semantic unease, because for twenty-five years one could frown at his splendidly unpunctuated message, 'Less fish meat bird cheese egg peas beans nuts and sitting', and somehow miss its drift. 'What exactly is your *beef*?' one might have asked him, hilariously, if one had only thought of it.

When Stanley Owen-Green started this anti-protein campaign in 1968, of course, food was not generally accepted as the enemy within, the way it is now. Devil-may-care people did not quip: 'I never met a carbohydrate I didn't like,' mainly because nobody would tumble the joke. In those crazy far-off days of prelapsarian ingestion, we bunged all sorts of things in our cake-holes and simply hoped for the best.

The idea of 'Protein Wisdom' in the late Sixties was revolutionary, therefore. Mr Green sincerely believed that too much 'married love' could kill, and that the way to banish its excesses was to reduce one's intake of fish meat bird. One only hopes he never popped into a picture palace to see Marco Ferreri's film *Blow-Out*, in the mistaken belief that it concerned the perils of Formula One.

But the trouble was, his placard was double-edged, both literally and metaphorically, and open to misuse. Ironically, those who positively embraced the notion of swooning unto easeful death sated with lust (not to mention nuts peas beans) knew from Mr Green's placard precisely which passion-packed items to add to their shopping lists.

What impressed everyone so much about Mr Green's

campaign, however, was not its faultless logic but its sheer constancy. After twenty years or so, a chap with a popular message might be expected to paint a new sign, take a new angle, jazz up the slogan; but Mr Green seems never to have done so. 'Less passion from less protein' was good enough to begin with, and good enough to end with, too.

Early reports suggest that the Museum of London will display Mr Green's placard, which is absolutely right and proper. By rights, I feel, he ought also to be inserted retrospectively into the works of Dickens. Thus, the last tremendous bustling-street sentence of *Little Dorrit* would read:

> They went quietly down into the roaring streets, inseparable and blessed; and as they passed along in sunshine and in shade, the noisy and the eager, and the arrogant and the froward and the vain, *and that man, you know, with the 'Less Passion from Less Protein' sign above his head*, fretted, and chafed, and made their usual uproar.

Fish have rights, you know. I learned this important piece of information last week as I was innocently travelling up an escalator at Tottenham Court Road, where aquatic matters are arguably furthest from a person's mind. But there it was, one of those little hand-written labels that fanatics attach to the posters; stating it quite plainly, 'Fish Have Rights'. Of course I laughed out loud – rights to what? fair trial? freedom of expression? abortion on demand? – but then stopped, confused. I mean, perhaps 'Fish Have Rights' was a joke. Or maybe it was the name of a really famous pop group. Worse, perhaps it signified nothing at all, but had been written by an unreconstructed surrealist, to see whether the word 'fish' in peculiar contexts still made people feel vertiginous and paranoid. In which case, I reflected (as I grasped the moving handrail for support), the experiment appeared to be working.

But it's all true. 'Fish Have Rights' is the latest thing in the anti-bloodsports campaign, and the British angler is the object not only of moral opprobrium but of sabotage attack. Really. There was a piece in the *Sunday Times*. Robert Redford has attached a disclaimer to his fly-fishing movie, *A River Runs Through It*, promising that no little fishies were killed, harmed, or even mildly disgruntled in the making of it, yet the 300-strong Campaign for the Abolition of Angling is still thinking to picket the cinemas ('This film degrades fish,' I suppose).

I had no idea of all this strength of feeling. Sitting quietly on a river bank under a big umbrella, thoughtfully masticating a cheese roll, our angler looks up in surprise to see a fully rubberized frogman advancing from the water, yelling that he is barbaric. Talk about surreal. What a way to find out that the first right of fish is the right to representation.

Personally, I could never love a fish. It is something to do with their short memories. Call me anthropocentric, but I refuse to lavish affection on a creature that, every few seconds, can't remember where it's seen you before. All aquarium-owners will gladly tell you that the extremely short memory-span of the fish is its great salvation in captivity, because while it endlessly circles its tank it supposedly thinks, 'Well, this is interesting; mm, this is interesting; gosh, this is interesting; corks, this is interesting.' But to me, that retention problem is a stumbling block to sympathy, and I doubt I shall ever march on Parliament with our amnesiac aquatic friends. 'What do we want?' we humans would shout. And the fish would give us that blank panicky look, as if to say, 'How do you mean?'

On the other hand, I do agree that it is odd to call angling a sport, when there is obviously never the slightest possibility that the trout will win. The great outdoors. Man against fish. Well, you have to admit that the contest is unequal. Moreover, the idea that a fish can outwit its predator ('Mister Carp was too clever for me today') is not much of a face-saver, in my opinion, and I am always surprised when people resort to it. But what really astounds me in this 'Fish Have Rights' business is that any sane person, looking around at the world's current brutalities, would put angling at the top of their activist agenda. Presumably they watch the news from Bosnia with their mouths open and their eyes all glassy, making little occasional 'Pup!' noises with their lips.

What it really boils down to, however, is that I just can't imagine the emotional dynamic involved in wanting to sabotage an angler. How do they get their dander up (especially once they're encased in a wet-suit)? Whereas the fox-hunt seems to have been designed in every detail to invite aggressive response (the horn! the horn!), I don't see how anyone could work himself into a lather about a bloke with a flask of tea in a fine drizzle being willingly outsmarted by a fish. It doesn't add up. It's like attacking a person for quietly reading a magazine. 'Look at him doing that! Ooh, that really makes me mad!' The drizzle scenario is like a red rag to a bull, apparently. Which is strange, of course, because in terms of unacceptable bloodsports, a red rag to a bull is really nothing like this at all.

☙

Attempting to cross a tricky road junction in south London recently, I was very nearly struck down by a speeding van. This is the sort of thing that makes me rather angry; in fact, had I not been carrying two heavily occupied cat-baskets at the time (one in each hand), I would have taken great pleasure in thumping the side of the van as it passed (sometimes the BANG resounds wonderfully). I still had the option, of course, of hurling a retaliatory cat-basket down the road after it, but luckily the thought did not occur to me until later. So, as I stood helpless on the tarmac, with the smouldering tyre-tracks running just inches from my feet, all I could do was squint at the receding vehicle in search of an identifying clue. And I got one. On the back of the van were two words I shall never forget: 'Bengal' was one, and 'Prawns' was the other.

As I sat in the vet's waiting-room and attempted unsuccessfully to comfort my shuddering cats by poking at them through the wire mesh of their baskets, it seemed to me that I had had a lucky escape. Nobody wants to be killed by a van; but it would be a great deal more irritating to be killed by a van with 'Bengal Prawns' written on it.

'How did she die?' people would ask.

'I think it was something to do with prawns.'

'But she never liked prawns.'

'I know.'

I couldn't help remembering that when Chekhov's body was returned to Moscow for burial, it was in a cart marked 'Fresh Oysters', but this inconsequential fact did nothing to lift my spirits, so I jiggled the cats for a bit and then hummed them a comic song until somebody asked me to stop.

I think about death sometimes. Analytically, of course. Recently, for example, I got together with a depressed friend, and we discussed – over a bottle of *crème de menthe* and a family bucket of Kentucky Fried Chicken – our views on suicide. It was jolly interesting. It turned out that our ideas were completely different, and that philosophers ought to have been brought in by the coach-load just to listen to us because what we said was so bloody profound. Her view, you see, was that whereas she often felt like killing herself, she didn't actually want to die. And I said, well that was so, so, amazingly funny, because whereas I often felt that I wanted to die, I didn't actually want to kill myself. We felt so proud of this extraordinary paradox that we treated ourselves to a large bottle of Bailey's Irish Cream.

Perhaps the 'Bengal Prawns' thing was a message; a presentiment. But what could it mean? Don't mess with prawns? One day you will die by prawns? You have taken the name of prawns in vain? I have no idea. But it turned out to be something of an epiphany, in any case; because, strangely enough, it has given me the will to carry on. No bloody prawn, I decided, is going to get the better of *me*.

Last autumn an Oxford man was prosecuted for strangling next door's parrot. You may remember the item in the news. The offending bird lived in a cage in the garden, the man had recorded piercing noises from it (up to 90 decibels), and finally it drove him berserk. It was a dramatic story, really, like something from a crack-up movie starring Michael Douglas. Man in specs yells, 'That's it! That's done it,' breaks down fence, wrestles with door of cage; parrot backs away uncertainly, squawking. Music soars; feathers flurry; shadows struggle; and a bird ladder is kicked over in the fight. The music drops to a low pulse, signifying that the grisly deed is done. The man falls back, stunned, stares at palms of hands. Then silence. The camera pans: empty perch, rocking swing, silver bell, mirror, scattered Trill, cuttlefish, end.

That's how I saw it, anyway. Here was a man pushed beyond endurance by the constant shrieks of a noisy bird (trained by its owners to squawk 'Mark', the strangler's name). And although I can't remember if he paid a terrible penalty for his crime, what I do remember is empathizing strongly with his frustrations, and thinking that the urge to strangle next door's parrot is probably one of the most passionate feelings shared by the silent outraged majority in this inwardly seething, overcrowded and latently violent country. Naked and raw, it is, the common urge to break the windscreen of a car whose alarm has been wah-wahing all night; to firebomb a house where a party never stops. Thank God they don't let us have guns.

And now we have the case of Diane Welfare, fined £12,500 last week for broadcasting Radio 1 to her neighbours, amid general cheers that something is finally being done. Hurrah, hurrah. If the court had also burst through the door shouting, 'That's it! That's done it!' and strangled the stereo or drowned it in the bath, I think I would be literally singing with joy. I don't care that Miss Welfare can't pay the fine. I don't even care that she is a teenage mother with a rotten life. When someone blasts noise at their neighbours, it is selfish and aggressive, and it drives you wild. It gets in your face. Nowadays when new neighbours move in downstairs from me, I cut the usual cheery preliminaries and just demand straight off to see the size of their speakers. Anything larger than a cornflake packet and my life is ruined. I will have to write in restaurants and sleep in the car.

A man next door to my mother drilled and hammered for two solid years, just beyond the four-inch dividing wall. 'Evidently he's fitting [WAR OOOUM, WAR OOOUM] tongue-and-groove pine panelling [whack, whack, whack] all round the living-room,' yelled my parents, grown pale and jumpy within a fortnight. Six months later, he was still at it. My parents went for walks, turned up the volume on the telly, and never complained because basically they were scared. Meanwhile, by their calculations, the driller ought to have finished going once round the room, so was presumably going round again. As the months turned to years and he didn't stop, we started to shake our heads and speculate. Either this man was a lunatic, or he had accidentally panelled across the doorways, and was now trapped for ever, drilling and hammering and adding planks, in an ever-shrinking upright coffin of his own construction. This latter hypothesis pleased us considerably, as it suggested the exercise was finite. Years in the future, we decided, he would be discovered by archaeologists and transferred to a museum still in his six-foot-thick pine box, perfectly preserved in a hammering position, with nails between his teeth.

You notice how neighbours of serial killers always gasp and shake their heads, 'But he was so *quiet*.' Too little is made of this insight, in my opinion; the point is missed. 'We never heard a peep.' 'We hardly knew he was there' – these are excellent character references, reasons for praying please, please give me a quiet psychopath next time. After all, neighbours come in just two varieties: those that are no trouble at all, and those that drive you bonkers because they are insomniac rap fans with speakers the size of stationery cupboards. Given the choice between Denis Nielsen and a rap fan as the person upstairs, you would certainly think twice before complaining about the drains.

I saw a woman tackled by a security man in a high street the other day. To be more precise, I heard her. There was a scuffle and a slap-bang as she hit the road, and then a scream, 'I'm so sorry! Please, I'm so sorry!' – at which point I looked around to see her, young and well dressed, bundled back into Marks & Spencer by a phalanx of strong arms attached to grim faces. The scene was electric – the culprit manhandled to her feet; the shocked onlookers; a plainclothes store manager barking 'Don't hurt her' – and was over in seconds. A routine apprehension of a shop-lifter, presumably, but it made all the hair on my arms stand on end. It was that shout of 'I'm so sorry!' that did it. 'Not much point being sorry,' I heard someone say, as the woman disappeared. Which seemed a bit hard, to me.

The thing is, people apologize a lot less than they ought to. It is as though saying sorry would cost them some vital bodily fluid; so they step on your toes and then glare at you instead.

'Your ornament got broken,' said the decorator the other week, matter-of-factly. He had been banging on a wall, you see, and the vibration had knocked the ornament into the bath, where it shattered. But although the word 'sorry' was definitely in the room, I was evidently the only person aware of it. I mournfully poked through the shards of porcelain, and stuck out my bottom lip. 'I was very fond of that,' I said. 'Were you?' he said in an arch sort of way, as though perhaps I shouldn't have been.

When you've got a name like Truss you just learn to apologize early on. I don't know. I'm sorry. But where was I, on that all-important first day at school, when everybody was told, 'And remember, kiddies: never apologize, because if you say you are sorry you accept personal culpability and can be sued for millions and millions of pounds'? Possibly I had stopped to apologize to someone. And then, when I sidled in, clutching my new leather satchel and saying 'Sorry I'm late', everyone marked me out as a muggins, for life.

Of course, motor insurance policies demand that we don't say sorry at the scene of accident, but I don't see why this should be taken as a rule of life. In any case, the insurance people don't tell us what to say instead of 'Sorry', if you are one of those sad specimens of humanity to whom the word comes naturally. Imagine you are negotiating Hyde Park Corner and you run into the car in front, all your fault, no doubt about it. Do you (as I did) forget all about the liability stuff, get out of the car and dance on the tarmac, flapping your hands and singing 'sorry-sorry-sorry-sorry' (to the amusement of the other driver, whose car is unscathed). Or do you take a deep breath and say 'Silly place to put a roundabout'?

I expect you are wondering what all this has to do with 'single life'. Me too. Except that I do seem to meet an increasing number of men who don't apologize, and I feel better off without them. Erich Segal never wrote a bestseller about it, but being single means never having to hear someone not say they are sorry. Which is nice. Perhaps my expectations are absurdly high, I don't know. But I used to have long-into-the-night debates with one chap, who staunchly upheld that if he did something to upset me *unintentionally* (lose my camera, for example) then apology was not appropriate.

'I was tired,' was the nearest thing I got to an apology. Once, when he was an hour late meeting me (and I was worried), he said merely, 'I washed my jacket, and had to wait for it to dry.' When someone says this to you, it is not only the word 'sorry' that hangs about in the atmosphere, crackling and sending off blue sparks. Unresolved aggression bounces off the walls and carpet in the shape of goats and monkeys. Frustrated to the point of tears, I would sometimes argue that the great merit of apologizing is that the apology can be accepted, and the whole thing forgotten. Somehow it is hard to accept 'I washed my jacket, and had to wait for it to dry' with any show of grace. And as you may see, I still have not forgotten it.

The only time you see public apology these days is in newspapers, when the threat of litigation (or the award of huge damages) forces them to say sorry – like small boys frog-marched to a neighbour's house and made to apologize for breaking a window. 'Sorry,' they mumble. 'Louder, please, and say it nicely.' 'Sorry.' And you know they are really all pinched up inside about having to do it. No politician will ever apologize to the homeless or to other victims of the recession, because apology is perceived to have an exclusive white-flag function – it means eat dirt, take the blame and be sued for millions and millions of pounds.

Whereas I have always taken apology to signify something else – an acknowledgement that, even unintentionally, you have caused somebody hurt. It is about *them*, not *you*. The woman who shouted 'I'm so sorry!' outside Marks & Spencer obviously had something to be sorry about, but I admire her nevertheless, because she might equally have shouted 'Fancy leaving all this stuff lying about, it's asking for trouble!' or 'I am postnatally depressed!' instead. If everyone took the line that either a) I meant to do it so I am not sorry, or b) I didn't mean to do it, so why the hell should I be sorry, the world will surely be a sorrier place.

⌒

Every year at about this time, I decide to enrol for a car maintenance evening class. No more will I be treated like a mug by unscrupulous garages; no more will I shrug and whimper – waving my arms vaguely in the direction of the bonnet – when someone asks if I have checked the oil. I will put my hair in a turban, talk confidently of nuts, and wipe my hands on a greasy rag.

So I buy my *Floodlight* adult education classes book and, grim-faced with determination, circle those dark oily satanic car maintenance courses. But then something goes wrong. I notice a flamenco class that's nearer home, or conversational Italian, or pastry cooking, and before you can say brakepads I have run smack into the crash barrier of my infirm purpose.

I mean, why fiddle with carburettors when you can make choux buns? Why probe a Fiat when you can pop along to the factory in Milan and say, quite casually: 'Piove da ieri sera' ('It has been raining since yesterday evening')? You can see the dilemma. If you took the flamenco, moreover, at least next time you had a dishonest mechanic to deal with, you could stamp your foot and flounce off with style.

I was reminded of all this by the new *Which?* report on MOT testing. Evidently the *Which?* team bought six crummy second-hand cars, all of them worthy of a fail, and submitted them for tests with six garages each. The results were reminiscent of the infinite number of monkeys – out of thirty-six tries, one got it right, but only by the law of probability. Most of the garages missed failure points; they also (as you might have guessed) failed things that were perfectly fine. *Which?* was not interested in the morality of all this, only in the problem of unsafe cars receiving MOTs. For the average punter, however, who writes the large cheque each year, her hand sweaty from shock, there is a larger investigation still to be done. To put it bluntly, these garages 'see her coming', so how about a controlled experiment? How about she takes her car in and waves her arms (bill: £300); and Nigel Mansell takes her car in instead, while she waits around the corner (bare test fee: £24)?

This is the world we live in, of course. If you are honest about your ignorance ('I know nothing about engines'), it is a point of honour that they should take advantage of you. Last year my car started making a ticky-ticky noise, like a sewing machine, so I drove to my usual MOT place and asked for an expert diagnosis. 'You'll recognize the ticky-ticky noise,' I said helpfully, 'It's the one that makes people look gloomy and say "tappets".' They stared at me, with big, giveaway £ signs flashing visibly in their eyeballs. Five hours later, I asked for a progress report. 'Just phoning around for a new engine,' they said, alarmingly. 'Pistons ... not worth taking the old one apart ... fifteen hours' labour at £28 per hour ... looking at twelve, thirteen hundred quid ... take eight days.'

I was stunned. Nothing in my conversational Italian had prepared me for this, not even 'Mi pare un po' (molto) caro' ('I think it is a bit (very) dear'). I said I would think about it, and retrieved the car, mainly because I could not face the tragic prospect of 'looking at' twelve or thirteen hundred quid, just to hug it once and say goodbye. Subsequently, of course, I was told by everybody – from taxi drivers to provincial mechanics to small boys on trikes – that the ticky-ticky problem was the camshaft, not pistons, and that the garage's mistake could not possibly be a genuine one.

Perhaps car maintenance should be placed on the national curriculum, alongside sex education. There is the same 'need to know', obviously. And perhaps I should just regretfully harden myself to the garage rip-off, and rejoice that the ethic of the grease-gun is not generally extended – or not so flagrantly – to other professions ('I think it's just a cough, doctor'; 'Nothing so simple, I'm afraid. In fact I'm phoning around for a replacement head').

Recently I saw an eight-year-old girl interviewed on television about *Jurassic Park*. 'Don't you think it will be distressing for you to see little children terrorized by dinosaurs?' the interviewer asked. 'But that's life,' piped the child. 'It would be silly to shield us from it.' She had a point.

Last Thursday, during the mid-afternoon power-cut that plunged the whole of central London into blacked-out, stuck-in-the-lift chaos, I decided to make the best of the remaining daylight by ferrying some paperbacks up the stairs to my office. We British, I pondered (as I balanced a pile of books in one hand and opened doors with the other), are so accustomed to dealing with the effects of other people's cock-ups – trains not running, post not arriving, delivery vans not turning up – that some people have stopped being angry, and instead take pride in the fortitude they show in such circumstances. Stuck in a tunnel somewhere near Victoria, they smile indulgently and award themselves medals for bravery in the face of overwhelming cock-up. This habit of shrugging at ineptitude is, I thought as I kicked one of the doors shut with a loud bang, precisely what is wrong with this bloody rotten stinking country.

Having my mind thus occupied with large thematic matters, therefore, I did not at first notice the presence of the two strangers who were following me up the stairs. Their brief-cases and nasty blue suits betrayed them to be businessmen heading for another part of the building, while their out-of-condition puffing and sweating gave them away as chaps who would normally prefer to take the lift. By way of pleasantry, I imagine, one of them tried to engage me in conversation:

'What have you done to the lights, then?'

'I beg your pardon?'

'What have you done to the lights?'

'Nothing to do with me,' I said.

'No, no,' he persisted, laughing. 'Don't give me that. I expect you plugged your typewriter into the wrong socket, didn't you, and blacked out the whole of London.'

Now remember: this was a spontaneous remark uttered to a complete stranger; and as such, I regard it as absolutely awe-inspiring. It is like seeing a perfect diamond: what *centuries* of top-quality British male prejudice it must have taken to refine a mind to such a pitch. This man had only to be presented with the situation of: a) the lift out of order; and b) a woman walking innocently upstairs minding her own business, and his mind instantly synthesized all of the following propositions:

a) all women are secretaries;

b) women are always to blame, whatever it is;

c) women are stupid about electricity, and are always blowing fuses by plugging their heated rollers into light-fittings;

d) women welcome gratuitous insults;

e) and even if they don't, there is not much they can do about it, because 'not being able to take a joke' is a feminine failing worse than sabotaging London's electricity supply.

This man believes all these things; he believes them, moreover, at a deep unconscious level. And because he believes them, he thinks he is better than me. How ironic that I learned all this during a power-cut.

Last week, in a branch of a well-known stationery shop, I had an interesting experience. It went something like this:

ME: Excuse me, I can't see any Amstrad ribbons. Could you … (*First Assistant points a finger at a low shelf, looks at me as though I am mad, and does not speak.*)

ME: Oh yes, silly me. Thank you very much. (*First Assistant does not react in any way, but then turns to friend and starts discussing lunch-breaks.*)

ME (*at till*): I'd like to pay for these please. (*Second Assistant silently picks up ribbons and rings up prices on the cash register. He does not announce the total, because of course I can see it quite as well as he can.*)

ME (*showing credit card*): Can I pay with this? (*Second Assistant wordlessly takes credit card and processes it, so that a bill is printed on the counter.*)

ME: Have you got a pen? (*Second Assistant points to biro next to the till; I sign. He fixes his gaze on the middle distance.*)

ME (*gathering up bag from the counter*): Well, I'll just take this, then. (*Nothing.*)

ME: Great. Lovely. Thanks. Bye-ee.

Now you could look at this scene in two ways. First, there is the 'lonely mad woman' scenario – you know, she's got her hair in plaits, she's got cat-dribble on her ankle-socks, and she's trying to engage healthy young shop assistants in banal conversation, hoping that this will relieve her feelings of solitude, and temporarily make her life worth living. Give her an inch, this woman, and she will produce a stack of photographs from her shopping-bag ('Here's a picture of a rice pudding I made last year'), and start saying 'Guess how old I am! Not bad for thirty-six!'

On the other hand, there is the argument that says a little bit of eye-contact never hurt anybody, and that however boring it is to say 'That will be £15.99' all day, it is an essential part of the job, and of the structure of civilization.

Even if young people cannot be trained to say, 'Can I help you?', or 'Did you see we had a new range of those?', I think there should be a sort of baseline of acceptable shop behaviour which would include: (1) announcing the total loudly enough for the customer to hear it, and (2) saying thanks for the dosh.

My own particular bugbears are bookshops (where I know what I want, and understand the system better than the assistants) and hi-fi emporia (where I don't know anything, but can, nevertheless, spot the tell-tale signs that my guess is as good as theirs). In bookshops I cunningly deploy my knowledge of the alphabet in order to go straight to the right place on the shelf; but if my book is not there, I ask. This is where I make my mistake. The assistant, looking slightly offended by my enquiry, slides off his stool, turns a key in his till with an audible huff, and heads for the wrong area of alphabet.

'Carter should be here,' I say, but he's not listening. He is trailing a fingernail along the Peter Ackroyds and Lisa Althers and pursing his lips. 'Actually,' I volunteer, 'Er ...'. But his concentration is impenetrable, as he works his way through Atwood, Barnes, Bowen, Boyd, Brink, Brookner and Byatt. Finding himself at Dibdin, he performs a few halting changes of gear between forward and reverse drive, until finally settling on the exact space where my finger is resting on the shelf.

'If it's not here, we haven't got it,' he announces, straightening up. After witnessing this ritual a couple of dozen times, you learn not to ask about any author whose name comes later in the alphabet than F, unless you are writing a thesis on alienation.

Sorry to go on in this old-codgerish vein, but since shop assistants are sometimes the only people I speak to all day, I am growing sick and tired of the rudeness. Hi-fi shops I only enter when I'm feeling particularly robust – and even then I try to cushion the experience by imagining that all the staff are blind. This helps a lot, actually. Blindness would excuse them from never looking you in the eye, from being completely unfamiliar with the stock, and from bluffing in transparent ways when asked technical questions.

'What does this button do?' you ask. The assistant looks at it in a vague, unseeing way, and says dismissively, 'Timer.' 'Oh, hang on,' you say, looking up from the instruction leaflet, 'it says here that it's a pause button.' The salesman shrugs, and diverts his attention to an argument at the other end of the counter, where a customer is demanding his money back until he is blue in the face.

I don't know what can be done about all this. I have started barking 'Howmuchdidyousay?' into the ears of people on tills, but only because it makes me feel better. My latest idea is to carry a little Sooty glove puppet, so that I can produce it at key moments and talk to it when nobody else is volunteering. 'What's that, Sooty?' I could say, next to the Amstrad ribbons, with Sooty speaking directly into my right ear. 'Down on the bottom shelf?' Sooty would nod his head in the traditional glove-puppet manner of bending three times sharply from the waist.

At the till, we could continue. 'Yes, Sooty? That will be £9.40? Allow me to lend you this biro? Thank you for your custom, and be sure to call again? Well, thank you very much, Sooty. It makes such a nice change from talking to myself.'

⌒

Remember the days of 'kitchen-sink drama'? Having grown up during the heyday of this raw, vigorous genre, I find now that its combined dramatic porcelain, taps and U-bends made a deep impression on me, as though dropped on my foot from a height. Placed in an unfamiliar BBC props room full of old white sinks, crude kitchen tables and Ascot water heaters, I feel sure I could identify them ('Arnold Wesker?' 'Shelagh Delaney!'), no problem. Around kitchen sinks, couples were always shouting and glowering at each other. They chucked plates and wrestled with the back door ('That's right! Go to yer fancy piece!') before storming out into the black night.

I was reminded of all this emotional turmoil when reading about a comparatively sedate organization called the Polite Society (patron: His Grace the Duke of Devonshire). The Polite Society is committed to maintaining everyday courtesy in British society and in particular believes machines have ruined our capacity for talk. The invention of the dishwasher, its manifesto says (with stars in its eyes), was a tragedy for domestic conversation, since washing-up was a matrimonial lubricant we could not afford to lose – 'The only opportunity man and wife may have to engage in comfortable small talk while she washes and he wipes.' A number of sweet bygone gender notions are enshrined in this pretty picture, but for the sake of brevity I think we'll let most of them pass. 'Oh look, here's a bit of old cornflake still stuck to the bowl, darling!' 'You're right, dear. Would you like me to commit suicide here at the sink, or shall I just pop myself upstairs?'

As a single person whose tea-towel never gets wet, I do see the point about the dishwasher, of course; it's no company at all. If you relied on it for anecdotes, you would wait a very long time. But if people don't want to talk to each other, surely the last thing that will cajole them into a pleasant gossip about the neighbours is a pile of greasy crocks. It is quite easy to wash up together without saying a word, both staring through the uncurtained window at the dark and rain, mouths set in a grim line. And another thing, if they are very keen on each other, surely this Mummy and Daddy would far rather fling those plates in the machine, push a button and retire to a more comfortable room? I was telling my friend Susan about all this wash-wipe nonsense, and she observed,

'Antony and Cleopatra didn't do the washing-up together, did they?' – an excellent point. The history of western civilization might have been quite different if instead of trying to impress his dusky Queen with the Battle of Actium, Antony had strapped a pinny over his leather skirt and made with the Brillo.

Machines certainly reduce the opportunities for everyday courtesy. If a door works automatically, you feel a fool holding it open; if you get your money from a hole in the wall, you shouldn't enquire about its Mum's new hip. On the other hand, this automation does protect the manners-sensitive among us from the irritation of finding doors dropped back in our faces, or speaking to a stooping bank clerk who shows us only the top of his head. What I mean is, nobody can behave badly around an automatic door; and it is rare to walk away from a cashpoint grumbling, 'That's the last time I go *there*.' The Polite Society dislikes also the way the Directory Enquiries service now starts off with a real person ('Which name? Which town?') and then switches to a computer voice with random vowels, preventing you from saying thanks. But looking at it another way again, at least this means that the operators don't spend all day exasperated by people hanging up *without* saying thanks. 'I don't believe it. I gave him the number and he just hung up.' 'That happened to me, too.'

Back at the kitchen sink, it's surely obvious that everything in the home is nowadays designed to make maximum time for the telly. That's just the way it is. People bicker about whose turn it is to load the dishwasher because there's a juicy kitchen-sink drama on the box. 'We are not Luddites,' says the Polite Society, 'but there is a danger that if we don't control technology, it will end up controlling us.' What a shame it's not that easy. I read this credo as it came off my Fax machine, and instead of just shouting 'Faster!' and 'Come on!', I tried saying 'Oh, thanks a lot' and 'Ta'. Imagine my surprise when it replied, 'You're welcome. And by the way, did you notice the new car outside Number 46?'

⁂

Hand me that legal aid application form. And lend me that pen. After years of cudgelling my brains for a suitable way of expressing my resentment at growing up in a house filled with tobacco smoke, I have finally hit upon the perfect solution. I shall sue them, take them to court, fleece them for every penny. Ha, let them put *that* in their pipes. According to the Sunday papers, children subjected to chronic passive smoking can now obtain legal redress for their long-term bronchial problems, and there will be a kind of wheezers' revolt. The courtroom picture is irresistible. I can see it now: the plaintiff (me) in the witness box, coughing delicately into a linen hanky, and pointing the bony finger of blame; and the rest of them in the dock, huddled together under a yellow mantle of tobacco smoke, doing a group impression of Auld Reekie with the wind in the East.

The only trouble with this happy fancy is that my case could easily be knocked down by a few simple questions from a skilled counsel. For example, were my family in fact ignorant of the dangers of tobacco smoke when I was a child? 'Yes, probably,' I mumble (into my sputum cup). 'A little louder,' they command. 'Yes,' I repeat. Did I ever encourage their smoking habits myself? 'I did,' I reply miserably. 'I bought them novelty ashtrays.' The judge raises an eyebrow, looks confused. 'For example, I bought an ashtray at the seaside shaped like a ram's head, with the words "For Butts" written on it. B U double T S. It was a pun, my lord. Also, I begged to be allowed to make roll-ups in a little silver machine. And whenever the Bob Newhart monologue about Sir Walter Raleigh's discovery of tobacco was broadcast on the Light Programme –' (here I break down in penitent sobs) '– I used to laugh with everyone else at the bit where he says "Don't tell me, Walt. You stick it in your ear."'

Passive smoking is something I feel so strongly about that I want to set fire to the tea-towels, yet strangely at the same time I find it impossible to make a stand about it retrospectively, especially on the home front. Will people really take their families to court? I don't believe it. How can you argue with people who, despite the advance of science, despite the warnings on the packets, and despite the fact that coroners now record smoking as a cause of death, keep puffing on the little white sticks and refusing to feel bad about it? Such fierce stupidity is intimidating. To the non-smoker, the behaviour of smoker families tells you quite unambiguously that if you've got a problem with this, then the problem is yours and you can keep it. If it makes you want to spit, then there you are.

So where my own relatives are concerned I do my smoking very passively indeed. While they light up repeatedly, I fantasize about strapping a battery-driven fan to my forehead, and yelling above the din, 'Can't hear you! Got the fan going!' – but unfortunately this helps only as a mental distraction. As a concrete act of defiance, I did once purchase an amusing T-shirt with a Larson cartoon on it ('The real reason dinosaurs became extinct' – showing a collection of prehistoric beasts furtively taking quick drags like schoolboys). But although I have worn this provocative garment twice to family gatherings, on both occasions I hastily obscured it with a jumper, so that it wouldn't cause offence or start a row.

Of course it is in the Bible, all this. 'The fathers have eaten sour grapes; the children's teeth are set on edge.' I don't remember how the next bit goes, but it's probably something like 'Tough banana, saith the Lord.' I am convinced that even the deity of the Old Testament, with his avenging tooth-for-a-tooth system of justice, would have advised against litigation in this case, on grounds of crushing futility. 'Car fumes are more dangerous,' say the smokers, airily; 'there is a higher chance of dying from a stray microwave.' Angry as I am about spending my school years feverishly coughing and hawking into lavatory bowls, I know what I am up against, and I know when I am beaten. If they won't admit they are poisoning themselves, these people, what earthly chance have I got that they'll admit to poisoning me?

This time last year I had never been inside a register office except for a wedding. Now I am a twice-over veteran of registering family deaths, and I feel I know all about it. The registrar meets you with a smile, invites you to sit at the other side of a desk, and draws your attention to a computer screen on which your answers will appear. You cling to an old brown envelope with 'Birth certificate' written on it in familiar handwriting, and experience a mixture of feelings, principal among them the terrible misgiving that your errand is a wicked mistake, and that your dad is going to be really dismayed and hurt when he finds out what you've done.

A couple of months ago, I took my second trip, this time to register the death of my grandmother. We followed the usual form. We were smiled at nicely, invited to sit down, referred to the same bereavement-friendly computer screen. It was a woman registrar this time, rather old-fashioned, with red fingernails, a frilly blouse and a tight suit. Nothing else was different; I sat in the same chair. I even found myself commenting gruesomely, 'This is just like last time,' as if I had wanted to see this room again ever in my life.

But here we were again, indisputably, and the heartbreakingly bare details of my grandmother's life (father's occupation: 'coal-heaver') were duly tapped into the computer. My mum, who was desperately upset, occasionally proffered extra details to swell the story, which made the registrar pause patiently with her fingers hovering above the keyboard, waiting to get on. Meanwhile I held mum's hand and stared glumly at the screen, making sure all the spellings were correct.

'Now, I'll just print out the death certificate,' said the registrar, tapping a few keys. And it was then that it happened. Somewhere between the instruction and the execution fell the shadow, and she suddenly got up, pushed back her chair, forgot we were there, and rapped hard on some frosted partition-glass. 'Brenda!' she shouted, in a great lather. 'It's happened again!' The smile had gone; there was something wrong. Mum and I looked at one another, perhaps to reassure ourselves that we had not actually disappeared.

The summoned Brenda burst into the room, in a blur of electric blue business suit, and rushed to the machine. 'What did it say?' she panted. 'I don't know,' panicked the registrar, wringing the manicured digits. 'Well, did it say "Disk full"?' demanded the fearsome Brenda. 'No, I think it was something else.' 'What did the man tell us to do?' barked Brenda, drumming her heels on the floor. We looked on, mum and I, wondering whether we should quietly leave, but guessing that it is probably a mistake to stop registering a death when you are halfway through.

What struck me most forcibly about this scene afterwards was that it could have come straight from an Alan Bennett play. Even the name Brenda had the right touch. How could this registrar not realize that by suddenly shouting 'Brenda, it's happened again' in the middle of a delicate transaction with grieving relatives, she was creating a scene that any drama critic would recognize from a dozen or more modern comedies? It was so strange. Perhaps she doesn't watch television. Perhaps she has no self-consciousness. Perhaps dealing with death takes away your sense of dramatic irony.

The last is certainly true. One of the dubious fringe benefits of your first significant bereavement is learning that the black-suited comic undertaker of popular imagination is not only the real thing, but that it isn't funny and you have to go along with it. You can't say, 'Can I have someone who wasn't in Joe Orton's *Loot*, please?', and you don't feel like laughing. Our two sets of undertakers have been ugly, seedy characters with dandruff, Brylcreem, ill-cut suits and nicotine stains who perspired in dark glasses as though rarely exposed to the light of day. And we sat there while they absurdly offered us a range of fancy caskets, knowing there was nothing we could do.

Stupefied by grief, you surrender. The arrangements for my father's funeral entailed an hour-long consultation with a jumped-up professional doom-merchant who actually wanted us to share the tribulations of the funerary business, even if it meant keeping us in teasing suspense. Can we have the funeral on Tuesday or Wednesday, we asked (wanting a simple yes). At which point he started waxing sarcastic about the unnecessary inconvenience caused by bank holidays, conjured up all sorts of distressing thoughts of coffins log-jammed on the memorial lawn, before finally announcing that he had already booked the crematorium for Wednesday at half past two. Sighs of relief and admiration all round. Our hero.

I understand now about Hamlet losing all his mirth. I used to think this meant he didn't laugh at jokes because he was upset. But I realize now that death is surrounded by dreadful comedy, which you are obliged to participate in, in the role of unlaughing stooge. Nigel Williams was told at the hospital that 'your father's not very well. Actually he's very poorly indeed. In fact, he's dead.' Well, it's all like that. Neighbours come round to tell you they are sorry, and end up compulsively relating (over several cups of tea) all the tragic bereavements in their own family, going back ten years. Dismayed, you can't believe they are doing it. Is this an Alan Ayckbourn play, or what?

The Trials of Celibacy Explored
with Surprising Frankness

The trouble with surprise spells of warm weather is that they make your thoughts run – rather inconveniently, in my case – in the general direction of sex. Damn and blast. What atavistic creatures we are, to be tweaked by the season in such an obvious way. You would have thought you could rise above it, in an age that can invent the multi-purpose bin-liner. Instead of which, all it takes is a small gust of warmish breeze ruffling the hair on the back of your neck, and the next minute you are startling pensioners at the Post Office by singing 'Gimme Gimme Gimme a Man After Midnight' while queuing for your tax disc.

Perhaps this is why the single person feels an enormous urge to spring-clean; it is Nature's way of turning surplus sap into a white tornado. 'Sub-Lim-Ate,' orders a croaky Dalek voice in one's head, and it seems wise to pay attention. Right, yes, get cracking. Eradicate the Sex Monster by sheer effort of elbow grease, and meanwhile pray for snow. As an additional precaution, remove any erotic element from your environment, such as Georgia O'Keeffe pictures (the ones that remind you of orgasms), and the Andre Agassi calendar you were so proud of. Deliberately avoid watching A Bouquet of Barbed Wire when it is repeated on TV Heaven, and put all your Gérard Depardieu videos in the shed.

But there is an old saying in my family: push sex out of the front door and it will come back through the plughole. 'Phew,' I said to the cats last weekend, when all this Superego activity was accomplished. 'Thank goodness I've dealt with *that* little problem.' But my sense of security was as ill-founded as Sigourney Weaver's in *Alien*. I leaned back in the bath and switched on *The Archers*, and jumped out of my skin. The Sex Monster was back! And it was running wild in Ambridge! I was aghast. Since when had *The Archers* been scripted by the ghost of Tennessee Williams? I silenced the radio in a bucket of water, but not before thinking that Jennifer Aldridge's 'trips to Felpersham' sounded nice. Damn and blast again.

So I was in a slightly jumpy mood when I went out for a drive on Sunday. On the run from both the Sex Monster and the Jif Imperative I ran straight into my nightmare combination of both – viz, the blokes with squeegees who haunt the traffic lights at Vauxhall Cross. Damn and blast for a third time. They come looming up at you unbidden, these johnnies; and then they clean your windows whether you like it or not. I had forgotten about them, because they disappear in the winter. But on the first warm day they rise up again miraculously, fully armed with buckets of water and beany hats. They are, I fancy, generated out of the swirling grit of Vauxhall by the mystical action of the sun, like crocodiles from the mud of the Nile.

Allow me to explain why I hate them so much. What happens is that having innocently drawn up at the traffic lights, you are approached by a man (or a kid) with a wet sponge, who is intent on washing your windscreen for a small fee. You mime a polite 'No thanks' but he is not deterred. You wave and swivel your palms in the internationally recognized signal for 'Leave it out, mate, and hop it', but he slaps the sponge on the glass, so that it dribbles dirty water across your line of vision. 'Bugger off,' you shout, but by this time he is wiping off the water, and you notice (at short range, through the glass) that he is the sort of person who breathes through his mouth, and wears the word 'Hate' tattooed on his knuckles.

Perhaps there are motorists who do not feel intimidated as I do; perhaps they say, 'Oh goody' and start rooting in their pockets for change. But perhaps they are not single women, frazzled by the challenge of suppressing their springtime libido, and crazed by the sea-change to *The Archers*. But it is a point of principle, in any case: if I say 'No' to these blokes, I truly believe they should leave me alone. To my mind, washing someone's windscreen against their will is quite as menacing as accosting them at a bus stop and insisting on manicuring their nails.

In the meantime, what is to be done about vanquishing the Sex Monster? Well, this week's plummeting atmospheric pressure has dealt with the immediate problem, thank goodness. I put the Andre Agassi calendar back on the wall yesterday, and I honestly feel OK. 'Chew string' was one helpful suggestion; also, 'Roll yourself in a length of carpet and recite *The Waste Land*' (apparently it works for some people). Back from my ghastly encounter with the Invasion of the Bucket Men, then, I decided to give the carpet-option a try, and it certainly helped. Despite gagging on the dust-balls, I found it amazing how Eliot keeps the Id firmly under wraps, while his unmistakable bass-line rhythm makes the whole experience so jolly:

> I think we are in rats' alley
> Where the dead men lost their bones
> There's not a soul out there
> No one to hear my prayer
> Weialala leia
> Wallala leialala
> Gimme gimme gimme a man after midnight.

Of course, a book about the IQ of cats begs a lot of questions to begin with. ('I am reading a book on cat IQ,' I mentioned to a friend. 'Short, is it?' she said.) But when you are a doting owner, keen to establish proof of your cat's outstanding native wit, you tend to lose sight of what those questions might be. So we sat down a week ago, the cats and I, and mutually ticked a lot of boxes in Melissa Miller's new *Definitive IQ Tests for Cats* (Signet, £3.99). The exercise produced quite fascinating results. I mean, according to our relative aggregates, one of the cats is cleverer than I am. Which is weird, really, because despite his mighty cat brain, guess who kept the scores?

'Look, kitty,' I said proudly, waving the book near his nose. 'You achieved 39 in visual skills!' But, alas, these visual skills did not extend to reading the printed page, or even getting the book into decent focus. Instead, he shrank back in evident distaste, as though the book were a custard pie. I tried another tack. 'Hey! Fur-face!' I yelled in his ear. 'You got 52 on audio abilities!' But strangely he seemed oblivious to my cry. 'And in social behaviour you got an amazing total of ...' However, my voice trailed off at this point because he had got up and walked out of the room.

If the cat is really cleverer than me, I just want to know one thing: why isn't he writing this article while I lie on top of the shed? But I suppose the answer is obvious when you put it like that. Cats are clever enough to get the better end of the symbiotic deal. 'Tell you what,' they say. 'You write the piece, and I'll sit on it. You earn the money, and I'll eat the Friskies.' In these circumstances, there is not much point attempting tests in verbal reasoning. ('Now let's try it one more time. STING is to THING, as STICK is to TH---.') A lot of nonsense is spoken about the cat's exceptional brain-to-body weight ratio. But when they introduced the concept of the electronic cat-flap, you may have noticed that they dispensed with the key-pad, because they knew that cats would need the number written down.

Miller emphasizes that her book of IQ tests should not be taken seriously, but I fear this is to misunderstand the character of her potential reader, which is bound to be fanatical and competitive. By means of multiple-choice questions, she tests your cat's intelligence in various situations – does it respond to its name, look with interest out of the window, hide things around the home, enjoy television? The trouble with such multiple-choice tests, however, is that there is a tendency in the respondent (me) to second-guess the top-scoring answer and automatically tick the appropriate box. Anyone who has doodled with a questionnaire in a women's magazine will recognize the syndrome.

> You are waiting all day and all evening for your new boyfriend to call. When he finally phones at midnight, do you:
>
> A: Break down in tears, explaining between sobs that you have become completely dependent on him?
>
> B: Wax sarcastic, and then yell that you never want to see him again, despite the fact that you like him very much?
>
> C: Act in a mature fashion, explaining that you demand respect for your feelings, and suggesting that he give you his phone number so that you can phone him next time?
>
> D: Not answer the phone, because you have just committed suicide.

Now, only a very thick person will not discern that C is the big-bucks answer here. Even if you spend your emotional life in a constant moil of sarcasm, yelling, bawling and throat sharpening, you will nevertheless be fully aware that the answer C will translate as the best personality type when you later consult the answers at the back. So, similarly, if you are filling in a questionnaire on your cat's IQ, and are asked the following question, you cannot ignore the temptation to respond dishonestly.

If your cat could read, which of the following newspapers would it probably buy?
A: Financial Times
B: Daily Mail
C: The Independent
D: The Sun

The fact that Cat No 1 is an obvious candidate for *Bunty*, while Cat No 2 would sit happily for hours with an out-of-date *What Car?*, is unlikely to deter you from ticking *Financial Times* with utter confidence, because you know it is the 'right' answer.

One thing I learnt from the book was that Sir Isaac Newton invented the cat-flap. It puts all his other distinctions in the shade. The prophet Muhammad, not wanting to disturb a sleeping cat, cut off part of his garment when he got up (bless his heart). Evidently the cat's special place in human affections (as well as its innate superiority as a species) is well attested historically, but I don't mind mentioning that I often pause wearily during essays on 'the cat in history' to ponder the famous *New Yorker* cartoon in which a man says: 'The fact that you cats were considered sacred in ancient Egypt cuts no ice with me.'

However, this book also contains modern stories of cats doing clever things – such as stealing bread from the kitchen and using it as bait for birds – which suggest the undeniable presence of functioning little grey cells concealed beneath the furry ears and eyebrows. Miller recounts one story of a cat which, having observed its owner's bleary-eyed wake-up routine of 'stick the kettle on, feed the cat', attempted to get things moving one morning by retrieving a used teabag from the bin and placing it on the owner's pillow. This shows amazing intelligence on the part of the cat, if only because it could remember key scenes from *The Godfather*.

Mostly, the way you define cat intelligence is by identifying things they won't do. Why is there no feline equivalent of Champion the Wonder Horse or Rin-Tin-Tin, Flipper or Lassie? Because a cat will not race into a burning building to rescue a baby, that's why. It is their own peculiar way of proving they are smart. In the heyday of the Hollywood studios, it was uncanny how those hopeful cat-hero scripts somehow always found their way to the bottom of the pile. 'Tiddles! Only you can save us! Squeeze through this tiny opening, and switch off the infernal machine! Go like the wind, and there'll be sprats for tea!' Some joke, obviously. 'Did somebody say infernal machine?' the cat says. 'Blimey, I'm off then.'

This book mentions that there were no cat skeletons found at Pompeii or Herculaneum, and jumps to the conclusion that therefore no cats lived there. But obviously they screeched out of town at the first whiff of sulphur. 'Tiddles!' they said in Pompeii. 'Only you can save us!' But a flash of cat bum was all that was visible, as the volcano rumbled and split. Centuries later, when the site was excavated, many petrified human bodies were doubtless found in the attitude of surprised cat owners calling to their pets in vain, frozen in time with boxes of Kitbits in their hands. Scrawled on a terracotta brick were some dying words in Latin which, roughly translated, meant, 'I don't believe it, the bloody cat has scarpered.'

As I explained earlier, Miller's tests for cats (the first half of the book) are fairly easy to second-guess. Once you have imagined that your cat's brain is entirely devoted to wangling the best deal for itself (and that it reads the FT), you are on your way to a hefty score. The second half is more tricky, however, because it is the test for owners, and the hidden agenda is more difficult to gauge. Take the following:

> Do you buy your cat something special for its birthday, Christmas or other special occasions?
> **A:** My cat is treated like any other member of the family.
> **B:** No. Cats cannot appreciate the significance of such gifts.
> **C:** Although I may remember my cat's birthday, I don't buy it anything to celebrate it.
> **D:** I'm not sure when my cat's birthday is, but I always include it in my own special celebrations, giving it extra food or buying it a special treat.

Well, I went for D, because it sounded the best – you know, affectionate without being fanatical. Also, I thought you could eliminate the others. Anyone answering B would obviously not be doing the questionnaire, being too busy running a cold, loveless reform school in a Victorian novel; while the person answering C is self-evidently too mean to buy the book. This only leaves A and D as decent cat-loving responses, and A sounded suspiciously like a trap for loonies. But A scored best, in fact. Because it turns out, in the end, that it is your level of fanaticism that is being tested.

Some of the questions concern how easily one's cat takes affront, and whether an owner will avoid saying anything negative (such as 'pea-brained') about a cat in its presence. Samuel Johnson, you may remember, had a cat called Hodge that he was fond of; and Miller quotes a wonderful passage from Boswell to illustrate the great man's sensitivity to the cat's feelings.

> I recollect my friend, when I observed Hodge was a fine cat, saying
> 'Why yes, Sir, but I have had cats whom I like better than this';

and then, as if perceiving Hodge to be out of countenance, adding, 'But he is a very fine cat, a very fine cat indeed.'

I think I prefer fine cats to clever cats. Which is my way of apologizing to my cats, should they ever read this. But imagine if your cat really were cleverer than you, and kept breezing in to say, 'Did you mean to leave that tap running in the bathroom?' and 'You really must read this TLS; it told me quite a few things about Tennyson that I didn't know.' Much better that they consider reading a mug's game and tap-regulation none of their business. All of this IQ testing makes you realize, with a sigh of relief, that brains are not everything.

The Single Woman Stays at Home and Goes Quietly Mad

To some people, Wimbledon is a tennis tournament. To me, it is a sort of binge. Confronted with a mere two weeks of fantastic tennis on the TV, I approach it with the same gimme-gimme intensity as the competition winner allowed three minutes to fill a shopping trolley with free food, or the fat boy attempting a speed record for the consumption of cream buns.

'More!' I demand, each evening at 8.15 when BBC2 stops transmitting, and the light begins to fade. The cats exchange glances, as if to say 'She's off,' but I take no notice. I want more, don't you see, more. More matches, more coverage, more – I don't know, *more male knees*. And above all, I want the very beautiful Pat Cash to remain prominent in the men's singles tournament, despite the unfortunate fact that he was knocked out last Thursday.

Bingeing, of course, is something you do on your own. It is therefore one of the great pitfalls of single life. When there is nobody to say, 'I think that's enough Wimbledon for one day,' you don't know where to stop. Leaving aside those knees for a moment, let's imagine you had an addiction to – I don't know, to fruit jelly, but did not live alone. Well, you would simply be obliged to curb those unnatural wobbly cravings, wouldn't you? It would be no good leaving a nonchalant bowl of Rowntree's black cherry on the coffee table, because the pretence ('We were out of olives, so I thought why not') would fool nobody.

But being single means that not only can you buy jelly in telltale catering quantities; you can make it by the gallon-load in the bath, and fill your entire living-room with great amber columns of it (if you want to), so that it resembles a confectioner's Monument Valley. Similarly, you can watch two channels of Wimbledon simultaneously, and then the evening highlights, and then your video of the highlights, without anyone objecting that it's getting out of hand. Believe me, it can happen. Last autumn I conceived a crush on an American leading actor and, in the absence of any restraining sensibility, had reached the jelly-columns-in-the-living-room stage before you could say 'Jeff'.

It was alarming. One minute I was quite normal, the next I was popping out to see Jeff's latest film every time I could contrive a free slot at 1.10pm, 5.05pm or 8.30pm. I considered finding out from *Mastermind* whether 'the films of Jeff' would be an acceptable specialist subject. And sometimes I pretended that I needed to cross Leicester Square on the way from Baker Street to Euston, so that I could accidentally find myself quite near the big Jeff pictures outside the Odeon. I was on a binge.

Virtually overnight, my flat turned into a 24-hour Jeff season-cum-masterclass. Friends popped in and found themselves being pushed roughly into seats while I snatched up the video control.

'Watch the way he says "Small world" in this scene.'

'Oh God. More Jeff.'

'Have I shown you the bit where he glances away to one side, and sort of rubs his nose before the "Listen, princess" speech? It's brilliant. The man's a genius.'

In the end, they gave up expecting me to talk about anything else; instead they patiently cut nice Jeff pictures out of magazines for me, bless their hearts. After all, we are each entitled to find our own peculiar way of dealing with celibacy, and it turned out that this was mine. Jeff. I was even happy. 'This is great,' I said. 'The last time I had a crush on someone it was in the pre-video age, but now I can watch Jeff deliver the "Small world" line fifteen times together if I want to.'

'Mmm,' they agreed.

And now it is Wimbledon, and I get so excited I expect tennis on all channels, all day. More. I get so involved that I even relish the on-screen computer statistics, tabling the number of times each player has changed his shirt or wiped his face with his wrist-band. In the old days, when Dan Maskell said, 'Seventh double-fault,' I would think, 'Oh crikey, what an old bore.' But now I exclaim, 'Seven!' and get angry with the commentators for making nothing sensible of such a thrilling statistic. 'Ah, now, seven double-faults,' said a Dull Donald during a match last week. 'Lucky for some, but perhaps just a passing statistic in a famous victory.' I could not believe it. 'What the hell are you talking about?' I yelled. 'Good grief!'

Thankfully the Wimbledon binge contains built-in limits, and will be over by Monday. I do not watch tennis at any other time of year: say the words 'French Open' and 'Prudential-Bache Securities Tennis Classic', and the pulse-rate does not lurch. It is the annual two-week tournament of Wimbledon – the stars! the knees! the knock-out! summer in the city! – that is so unputdownable. It makes me think of warm summer fairs and dances in Thomas Hardy; the travelling circus setting up tents for solstice-week on some pagan hillsite, and the whole town queuing up nightly on hot dusty grass to grab it before it goes. I am getting carried away, I suppose. But honestly, for an all-alone binge, Wimbledon is almost as good as sculpting indoor jelly stacks. And a lot less messy.

What does it mean, anyway: 'Do not remove lid before cooking'? There you are, in the kitchen, cook-chill dinner in your hand, oven nicely heated to 180 degrees, saliva glands triggered to the point of no return, and you receive this gnomic instruction about the lid which stops you dead in your tracks. Does it mean take the lid off, or don't take the lid off? Why does life have to be so complicated?

'I'm cooking it *now*,' I reason (I have to talk it through, slowly, usually sitting down). 'And I didn't take the lid off *before*. Which was *right*. Hmm. All right so far, then. So perhaps I should take it off *now*. But perhaps they mean not to take it off until *after it's cooked*. But then of course I *will* take it off when it's cooked, won't I, ha ha, because otherwise I *couldn't eat it*. Hmm. So why would they mention it? I mean, if I didn't take the lid off *then* I'd have to throw it away uneaten, and all that cooking would have been a waste of time. Hmm. And they show a serving suggestion on the box, so they can't mean for you not to get the food out, otherwise they'd show a picture of a foil box in *a bin*. Hmm. And another thing ...'

This goes on until the ghost of Bertrand Russell whooshes through the kitchen (screaming what sounds like 'For Pete's sake') and dashes the box to the ground. It's usually Russell, but sometimes it's Wittgenstein. I have lost a lot of dinners that way.

As a consumer, one often finds oneself on the receiving end of superfluous advice, and I suppose it is a measure of one's mental health how one deals with it. Buying a couple of ice-cube trays the other day, for example, a friend of mine discovered an interesting household tip on the packaging: 'Keep a tray in the ice-box for those occasional drinks, and keep another in a chest freezer in case of unexpected callers or a surprise party!' Could have worked that out for myself, thought my friend – but then she is a sensible, well-adjusted person who does not experience semantic vertigo over the removal of tin-foil lids. A more neurotic and literal-minded consumer (i.e. me) would have read this ice-tray advice on the bus home, and been obliged to go back to buy a chest freezer.

My hobby, by the way, is replicating serving suggestions. You know: I study the picture on the packet and re-create it with the real food. It is an unusual and creative pastime, I like to think. Sometimes, with a frozen dinner, the serving suggestion seems to be that you just take the food out of the dish and put it on a plate with a sprig of parsley, which is a bit too easy and not much of a challenge, quite honestly. But sometimes you have to add new potatoes or peas or something, and a bottle of wine in the background on a chequered tablecloth, and then you can spend quite a lot of time getting the composition just right. I have never told anybody this before.

Sometimes, just for a change, I defy the consumer recommendations. For example, recently on a bottle of hair conditioner I came across the advice: 'And then just arrange your hair in its usual style!' And I thought, well, I shan't then, and I put my head in a bucket instead. I thought the advice was slightly redundant, in retrospect (from inside the bucket). I mean, if they hadn't said anything I would have arranged my hair in its 'usual style' without even thinking about it. I wonder how they know where to draw the line, these people. Perhaps there are other bottles which advise, 'Arrange your hair in its usual style, and then have a nice cup of cocoa'. Or, 'Arrange your hair in its usual style, and then take a holiday in the West Country'.

Some manufacturers of prepared meals tell you that, after cooking, you should empty contents on to a plate. Before long they will also tell you to eat contents, burp (optional), wash up the plate, turn off the lights and lock the back door before going to bed. People are not being credited with much initiative, it seems to me. But then I am clearly susceptible, because I read all small print, listen to all advice. 'Serve chilled,' says the gazpacho carton, so I go out and stand in the rain without a hat. The strange thing is that when I come back in, the last thing I want to eat is some cold soup.

Recently I read some advice for people living on their own. I thought it would be about creating a helpful mental attitude, but it said things such as 'Don't open the door to strangers' and 'Have baths on a regular basis'. I was reminded of a student journalist who once shadowed me for a day and who told me that the lecturers on the journalism course had given her some pretty good advice. 'What do they tell you to do when you interview somebody?' I asked, hoping for some useful interrogation tips. 'Well,' she said, 'they say don't forget to take your bus fare. And always have a sandwich with you in case of emergency.'

So that's it, then. I don't open the door to strangers, and I keep taking the baths. I arrange my hair in its usual style, and I empty contents on to a plate. I carry a sandwich at all times. It's all you can do, really. I remember that I used to pass a doorway on the way to work each day, where I saw a little sign: 'Speak into the microphone.' And even if I was late, I would say 'Oh, all right then,' and think of another old Max Miller routine to regale it with.

In the early 1980s, when I was a compulsive *Blue Peter* viewer (recording it while at work, and priding myself on not missing a single show), there was a very upsetting Thursday evening which I shall never forget. There I was, safe in the usual items (potted biography of Louis Braille narrated by Valerie Singleton; how to make a Dinky Toy car-park out of a cornflake packet and a drinking straw), when suddenly Simon Groom announced brightly, 'And today we reach the letter M in our Dogs' Alphabet.' I felt as though my entire world had been tugged from under me. Did he say 'Dogs' Alphabet'? What Dogs' flipping Alphabet was this, then?

I remember standing up abruptly from my working-girl TV dinner, and spilling jelly and custard on the carpet. I choked on some hundreds-and-thousands. I was so outraged that I virtually ignored the ensuing scenes of a large mastiff dragging a *Blue Peter* presenter skidding across the studio floor, knocking over those triangular stands with teddies on, amid reassuring shouts of 'Ha ha, everything is under control.' I was too angry to enjoy it. 'When did you do the letter L?' I shouted, in a sneering tone. 'Nineteen seventy-two?'

So it is with some trepidation that I announce that today we reach the letter H in our Single Life role-model series. Ahem. The choice is wide: Heidi, Miss Havisham, Hinge and Brackett, Harvey the six-foot rabbit. Oh yes. Each tells you so much about the advantages of the unmarried state – in which you can be mad, Swiss, invisible or purely imaginary, and can run around with your hair on fire. But actually I have invented the Single Life role-model series because I want to discuss the little silhouette woman in *Hello!* magazine who illustrates the films-on-TV page, and she is such a strange phenomenon that I couldn't see how else to bring the subject up.

She speaks to me, this lonely figure; I don't know why. Next to the review of each film appears this little illustrated woman, who is evidently watching the TV from a firm 1960s low-armed chair in an empty room. She is wearing outdoor shoes and a knee-length skirt, and she is reacting with bold body language to the quality of the films she is watching. I can imagine her watching that famous *Blue Peter* episode alongside me, and expressing the whole thing more eloquently, and without words – a hand cupped to her ear ('What's this?'); her arms folded in front of her ('I don't believe it'); she shakes a fist ('Someone will pay'). She is a mime, you see, this woman. Her body is her tool.

Her role is this. When the film is very good, she stands up and applauds enthusiastically; when the film is entertaining she leans forward, resting her elbows on her knees and her chin on her hands, possibly holding her breath. When it is only fair, she sits back, with her hands in her lap. And when it is boring, she sticks her legs out and flings back her head, as though she has been shot.

I have some quibbles with the authenticity of these reactions, of course. Personally, I lean forward with my head in my hands when the TV is terrible, not good. I jump out of my seat only when I want to ring up *Blue Peter* and give it a piece of my mind. When the telly is exciting, I lie back happily with a cat on my chest; and when it is excellent, I slide down so far in the chair that the only thing vertical is the top half of my head.

But the compelling thing about this woman is not the form but the intensity of her reactions. She concentrates without let-up, whether the stuff is good or not. In the course of a week's films she leans forwards, leans back, stands up, claps her hands, gets shot, leans forward and leans back – but she never stops watching. Why did *Hello!* choose this figure? I suspect because she is the antithesis of the couch potato. She is slim and active and self-possessed, and she would never be caught dribbling hot Ribena down her neck by trying to drink it without sitting up – which is what I do, now I come to think of it, while reading *Hello!*

She gives the lie to all those worthy sociology projects, in which closed-circuit cameras are rigged up next to people's television sets, to observe how broadcasting is treated in the home. Through the fishy lens, you see the ghostly figures of Mum and Dad wandering in, reading the paper, blinking stupidly at the screen while exciting car-chase noises and gun shots emanate from it, and occasionally pointing at the picture and saying, 'I know that bloke. He was in, you know, whatsit-called. Yeah, he was,' before wandering out again.

I have never seen one of these experiments applied to a person who lives alone, but I think it would be rather different, and a bit disturbing, because of the aforementioned intensity of response: 'What Dogs' flipping Alphabet?' 'God, I *hate* Noel Edmonds!' 'Why are the weather forecasts so *short*, for heavens' sake!' 'They'll never get a self-respecting Dinky car in a car-park made out of cornflake packets!' and so on.

I have great hopes for this woman in *Hello!* I feel she has room for development, and an obvious life of her own. Her little figure could start popping up elsewhere in the magazine, responding to the articles with exaggerated yawns while reading in the bath, or peering terribly closely with a magnifying glass at the telephoto pictures of the King of Spain.

And sometimes, of course, she could fling the magazine aside, turn off the TV, kick off the sensible shoes, and perform the polka with the cat in her arms, the way ordinary single people do. Go for it, my little friend. Live a bit.

⟨⟩

A telephone rings. It is tea-time on a day in late June. England. The columnist (a harmless drudge) hastily presses the 'Mute' button on her television remote control. The giveaway background noise of 'Pock, pock, applause, Thirty love' abruptly ceases. She grabs the receiver.

COLUMNIST (*defensively, and without punctuation*): Hello who's that of course I'm working good grief up to my armpits in fact Huh do you think I've got nothing to do but watch tennis? (*Her voice rises to a squeal.*)

There is a pause, while the caller lets the hysteria subside.

FEMALE FRIEND: Psst, it's me.

COLUMNIST: Linda? Oh, thank phew for that. I was just watching Wimbledon.

FRIEND: I know, so was I. Did you see him? Andre the Adorable, did you see him?

The columnist guiltily surveys the Andre Agassi press cuttings littering the floor of the study, and nods dumbly. She has just finished entering the names of today's winners in the special men's knock-out tournament chart. A keen-eyed observer would note that the equivalent chart for the women's tournament is left curiously blank. Taking a deep breath, she makes a decision.

COLUMNIST (carelessly): You mean the Agassi match? Oh, I believe I did just manage to catch every single minute of that one, yes. Mmm. I was particularly impressed, actually, by the champion's new short-action serve – 118 miles per hour he's getting – the power of the ground strokes, top-spin, all that. 'Ooh, I say,' as Dan Maskell used to exclaim, ha ha. Oh yes, French Open, lob, tie-break, Gabriela Sabatini.

FRIEND: Lynne. You're talking funny. Can't we discuss chest hair, like we usually do? Is there somebody there?

COLUMNIST: Good heavens, no. It's just that all these technical sports-reporter aspects, none of them passes me by. More like a fly-swat than a serve, I'd say, that new Agassi action, but still 118 miles per hour. Amazing. Sport can be really interesting, can't it? Can't think why I'm usually so dismissive of it. Also, there's these new, um, graphological racquets ... and, um, did I mention 118 mph, and the linesmen, gosh, Sue Barker, new balls, fascinating. And on *Today at Wimbledon*, Humphrey Carpenter can't even say 'Ivanisevic' properly! So what makes me cross –

FRIEND: You mean *Harry* Carpenter.

COLUMNIST: What?

FRIEND: Not Humphrey Carpenter.

COLUMNIST: Well yes. Yes, obviously. So anyway, what makes me cross is this. Here we are, you and I, having this highly informed and sophisticated conversation about the ins and outs of grand slam tennis, and the papers insist that when women become obsessed with Wimbledon, it's only because of the so-called hunk factor, because of the gorgeous pouting well-built athletic blokes such as Michael Stich and Goran Ivanisevic and – sorry, can't go on, throat a bit dry. Anyway, the idea is that we're watching the legs and the midriffs, not the tennis, I mean, that's absurd, obviously?

FRIEND: Eh?

COLUMNIST: Absolutely absurd.

Pause.

FRIEND: But they've stopped showing Andre's midriff, in any case. I phoned up yesterday to complain.

COLUMNIST: You did? Good for you. I mean, I hope you also mentioned their excellent coverage of his stunning returns of serve, and inventive cross-court passes?

FRIEND: No, I didn't. I said, I am a licence payer and if I want to see the dreamboat's tummy, the dreamboat's tummy I shall see.

COLUMNIST (*struggling, but steadily losing her grip*): Gosh. Whereas me, well, scoreboard, let-cord judge, first service, Cyclops –

FRIEND: Give it up, Lynne.

COLUMNIST: Shall I? Drop-shot, foot-fault, er ... Are you sure?

FRIEND: Definitely.

Pause.

FRIEND: I see Lendl got knocked out, then.

COLUMNIST (*resigned but happy*): Never fancied him, myself.

FRIEND: Nor me. Great player, I suppose?

COLUMNIST: No, no. Something to do with those stringy legs and the unattractive way his socks stayed up.

FRIEND: I know exactly what you mean.

I was interested to read in last Monday's paper that a possible side-effect of low-fat diets is an increase in aggressive behaviour, especially since I have now reached the stage in my own low-fat diet where I would happily mug somebody for a small sliver of cheese. Aggressive, eh? Take off your glasses and say that. It is the sort of story that makes you uncertain; it muddles things up that were previously clear. Was I being aggressive when I forced copies of Rosemary Conley's *Hip and Thigh Diet* on unwilling friends, instructing them to read it (or else)? I looked back with a sad little smile to the innocent days when I could say that the only drawback to low-fat diets is that they make you quite thin, thus making it difficult to store pencils in the folds of your torso.

But now, it seemed, there was one of those pesky little hormones to be considered – a hormone moreover that refused to be secreted to the brain unless there was sufficient cholesterol around, the upshot of which might be a propensity for violence. 'Bastard,' I said, involuntarily. I scoured the rest of the paper for supporting evidence (linking murders with Ambrosia Low-Fat Rice Pudding) but was disappointed. There was no statistical survey showing that the people who knock off policemen's helmets invariably prefer St Ivel Gold to butter in a blindfold test. I suppose we shall just have to sit back and wait for the inevitable confirmation of the story from the American law courts. It cannot be long, surely, before the first serial killer is acquitted by an American jury on the grounds of diminished responsibility (by reason of cottage cheese).

In my own case it is hard to establish any straightforward cause and effect, since I started the low-fat diet simultaneously with embracing the single life. Any character change, therefore, might certainly be the result of pizza deprivation; but on the other hand, perhaps I have just been unhinged by the burden of sole custody of the cats. The causal borderline is murky. I have noticed, though, that I get extraordinarily jumpy and irrational in the vicinity of high-fat food. For example, the idea of eating crisps now alarms me so much that in Sainsbury's I remove them surreptitiously from other people's shopping trolleys, and scuttle off to hide them in the bin-bag section. The fight against fatty food has become a personal mission. Yesterday my next-door neighbour mentioned that she is partial to a spot of Camembert and I reacted with such horror that she might have said she enjoyed jumping in front of tube trains to test their braking distance.

The only way to set one's mind at rest, I decided, is to do a bit of independent research. Follow a clamping unit around central London, for example, and offer cubes of lard to people whose cars have just been immobilized. 'Do not attempt to move it!' I might chuckle, springing out from behind the clamped car and proffering a platter of Cookeen-on-sticks. 'I wonder if you would be interested in taking part in a little survey I am doing?' I can imagine some interesting results. Or I could attend the check-out in Sainsbury's (surrounded by people saying, 'Funny, what happened to the crisps?') armed with a tub of low-fat yoghurt and a packet of pork scratchings, so that I can nibble little bits from each, monitoring my reactions. I could stand there with my hand on my head saying, 'Which way? Which way?'

The check-out is the right place for the experiment because while other people seem undisturbed by the sight of their shopping hurtling serially towards them down the conveyor belt and slamming into a multiple pile-up at the end, I loathe the avoidable frenzy and entertain visions of clonking the check-out lady on the head with a tin of Felix to slow her down. The only trouble is that, what with all the frantic packing and sweating and muttering, I shall probably forget to eat the pork scratchings. I get too worked up, really; and I don't suppose diet is the answer. Either supermarkets must adopt the American system of packing the bags for the customer, or the government must relax the gun laws. The question: 'Could you work more slowly please?' would pack a lot more punch if backed up by a loaded .45.

Last week's article was not only concerned with violence; it also suggested that low levels of cholesterol could be linked to unsuccessful suicide attempts. Great. Wonderful. First class. I am reminded of the time an editor said to me: 'Perhaps you could just be like Dorothy Parker,' and I misunderstood. What, keep slashing my wrists and drinking shoe polish? Keep waking up in hospital to hear wisecracking friends say: 'You've got to stop doing this, or you'll make yourself ill'? If this low-fat existence offers the fate of Dorothy Parker, perhaps it is time to reconsider. After all, even the exciting prospect of death by spontaneous combustion (which I've always fancied somehow) is less inviting from the low-fat point of view, since one's body would burn for a considerably shorter time than would make the option properly worthwhile.

❧

In my flat, I have a small flight of steps, and it worries me. Because one day, in a blur of windmilling arms and high-kicking legs, I am convinced it will shape my end. In itself, this staircase looks innocent of hazard: there are no loose stair rods, and if ever I discover ball bearings, bars of soap, or sheets of slippery tin-foil on the top step, I clear them carefully before starting my descent. No, the trouble is, these stairs lead to the kitchen – and anyone who lives with cats will instantly grasp the nature of my fears. For whenever a cat hears someone heading, with a loaded tray, in that direction, he looks up, thinks quickly (but not deeply) – tins! cat-bowl! tea-time! – and makes a blind dash, in the manner of a furry bowling ball hurled with gusto down an alley. There is a heavy expectant pause as he thunders targetwards, and then *crash* – the pleasant hollow sound of stricken skittles is reluctantly simulated by the windmilling lady with the tray.

My only consolation, as I await this disaster, is to muse (albeit tautologically) that 'most domestic accidents occur in the home'. And how right I am. A recent DTI report about domestic mishaps evidently included the extraordinary statistic that twenty-nine people last year were injured by dressing-gowns, while six named place-mats as their personal Waterloo. Yes, place-mats. Adjust these numbers upwards to account for people too proud to admit to misadventure by warm fluffy towelling or slim cork rectangles and we can see the extent of the danger in our homes. But how was it that 101 people fell victim to their own trousers? How was it that a lone peculiar person was afflicted by a tea-cosy? Crime novelists must be in ecstasy at the news. Suddenly it is permissible for a suspicious detective to peer quizzically at a lifeless body, suck his teeth, and say, 'Of course, this *may* be just a straightforward tea-cosy casualty, but I rarely trust the most obvious explanation.'

Ah yes, trousers, dressing-gowns, bread-bins, place-mats, tea-cosies, slippers – all those innocent Christmas gifts now carry the unfortunate connotation of the loaded gun. Personally, I find myself wondering (with a feverish urgency) what sort of place-mat. I mean, the rough raffia sort could give you a nasty scratch, I suppose; and the smooth laminated hunting-scene sort might possibly raise your blood pressure if you were an animal-rights activist. Neither, on the face of it, could land you in hospital.

No, only one explanation will satisfy all the scrappy data at my disposal: that instead of umpteen implausible domestic accidents taking place last year entailing tea-cosies and slippers, there was just one enormous out-of-hand Christmas party involving 101 drunken people spilling on to a main road wearing their trousers on their heads, and six attempting to skate across a frozen swimming pool with place-mats strapped to their feet. It's the only solution that makes sense. 'Let's break into the dressing-gown warehouse,' yells someone wearing a knitted tea-cosy as a balaclava, twenty-nine people following behind him, stumbling. But alas, once inside, blinded by the tea-cosy, he falls against a lever, and from a great height a large bundle of dressing-gowns promptly plummets towards their unwitting bonces. Meanwhile, back at the party, the innocuous game 'Toss the slipper in the bread-bin' has been proceeding safely until somebody has the bright idea of transferring the action downstairs to the kitchen. At which point a cat wakes, looks up, thinks quickly (but not deeply), and – well, you can guess the rest.

The DTI does not investigate the statistics, just tabulates them, so it's no use asking for the true story. Presumably most people made their statements in a state of shock and blamed the wrong thing. 'Why did you fall downstairs, madam?' 'The tray!'

A friend was once waiting in an uphill queue at traffic lights when her car was threatened by a van in front, slowly rolling backwards. Having honked her horn in vain, she ran to the driver's door, and discovered a woman piling plates on the dashboard. Evidently, they had slipped off; hence the neglect of the handbrake. 'Plates!' she laughed, by way of inadequate explanation. 'But they're all right, luckily.'

☞

A few years ago the American magazine National Enquirer ran a very helpful tip-list entitled 'Ten Ways to Spot Whether Your Grandparent is an Alien'. Evidently a large number of American teenagers were racked with worry on this issue and required some official guidelines for confirming or allaying their suspicions. So the Enquirer did its civic duty, telling youngsters to peel their eyes for certain telltale signs. 'ONE,' it blared, 'Gets up in the night for a glass of water. TWO: Remembers things from long ago with clarity, yet can't summon up details of yesterday afternoon. THREE: Takes naps.'

The article did not explain what dastardly mission these alien wrinklies had been sent to Earth to fulfil, so naturally one formed one's own theory on the available evidence. Clearly they came here in their silver shiny spaceships with the sole intention of putting their feet up and grabbing forty winks. Independent evidence backs up this notion. For as any astronomer will gladly affirm, very few comfy chairs have thus far been sighted on the surface of Alpha Centauri.

I mention all this because, according to a bizarre item in *The Times Magazine* recently, the American passion for aliens has not declined. True, the *National Enquirer* no longer carries those entertaining whole-page adverts for genuine extraterrestrial mineral samples (actual size) ostensibly brought back by Wyoming women from adventures in hyperspace. But apparently a new American movie in which a spaceship abducts a humble logger from Arizona (keeping him five days) is billed on its posters as 'Based on a True Story'. It pulls you up short, this kind of thing. I mean, leaving aside the objection that it *can't possibly be a true story*, doesn't anybody stop to ask why superintelligent aliens would do it? I mean, what's in it for them?

It ought to be a source of national pride that in Britain we don't automatically think in terms of aliens. The 'Lord Lucan Spotted in Sea of Tranquillity' story, accompanied by fuzzy aerial photo, somehow fails to grab our imagination, which should be cause for whoops of joy. Brits who abscond from work will possibly resort to far-fetched tales of illness or amnesia, but rarely do they claim to have spent a week in a spaceship unable to phone the office because the aliens (ironically) hadn't heard of Mercury.

'So where've you been?'

'Well, with aliens.'

'Oh.' A pause. 'Was it good?'

'Fine, yes. We did some crop circles. They've got a special attachment.'

'What were the aliens like?'

'Funny. They slept a lot, and kept asking me to remind them who I was, and then occasionally they got up for a glass of water.'

Just why America is more susceptible to 'true-life' alien stories is hard to account for (at least without being offensive) but it obviously entails a childish confusion about religion and space – which is a reasonable mistake, I suppose, since both originate in the sky. Visitations from the universe are the new-world equivalent of weeping statues in Catholic Europe, and in traditional American space movies, the identification of the visitor with the Messiah is so complete as to be almost laughable. In John Carpenter's film *Starman*, the alien comes in peace, is persecuted, raises the dead and ascends on the third day in a blaze of light. The fact that he also samples apple pie ('Terrific') and wins half a million dollars in a casino does not detract from the analogy, it simply confirms that this is messianism American-style.

Of course, the ludicrous feature of the aliens-from-space belief is that it expects these visitors to take a wise, fair and godlike interest in the way we are running our planet, when it is more likely (as Woody Allen once pointed out) that they will just turn up one day and dump their laundry – socks, underpants, shirts, jackets – with instructions to have it ready by Thursday. Meanwhile they will settle down in front of our TVs for a mass alien after-dinner snooze. Another fond illusion bites the dust, but still, it's only the same lament that has resounded through the ages. We ask for bread, and they give us stones; we ask for gods, and they give us ironing.

After the price of Whiskas and the paucity of NatWest Servicetills in the Marylebone area, my favourite conversational topic is garden sheds. I can wangle them into any kind of interchange – from the anecdotal ('Roald Dahl? Writes in his shed, you know'); through the philosophical ('But how can you tell your shed is *still there* when it's night-time and *you can't see it?*'); to the seductive ('I'll just pop down to the shed and slip into something more comfortable'). I am, you see, hoping that people will ask me to tell them more about my shed. But, strangely, no one ever does. The other day I even (Oh God, did I really?) tried to 'talk sheds' with Melvyn Bragg.

Perhaps one day someone will put together a glossy book called *The South London Shed* and ask me to write a little piece: about when my shed was built, what additions I've made, and how I sit in it all day wearing a straw hat and watch other people do the gardening. But I doubt it. That sort of request goes to the idle rich, like the people who have contributed to *The English Garden Room*, edited by Elizabeth Dickson (Weidenfeld £8.95). Never have I been more troubled by a large-format paperback. For it has made me discontented not only with my shed, but with my entire lot in life.

It must be said that the book is full of stunningly beautiful photographs. Conservatories are lovely places: huge and healthy plants set against cane furniture, stone paving, tall jardinières, classical statuary, and the odd piano – you can't go wrong. Lady Aberconway has a large rectangular pool in hers. 'The surface of the pond,' says the caption, 'unites by its reflection two convex shapes in perfect harmony.'

But it's all this harmony that's so upsetting. All this tranquillity and all this leisure to enjoy it. I can't bear to think of it – that some people actually have the time to swing in hammocks. Or is that just an illusion fabricated for the book? Perhaps Princess Nicholas von Preussen is really just as driven as the rest of us – hanging about in the vet's waiting room with her dachshund (Lily); getting into the slowest queue in Sainsburys. The most violent envy I have ever felt goes out to Mary Douglas-Scott Montagu, who spends her summer months playing Wendy House in a showman's caravan in the grounds of Beaulieu. She collects up the family pets and a couple of good books and 'lazes around'. 'It is the most luxurious and magic escape from the mundane pressures of everyday life.' Huh.

Perhaps this is what such publishing is for: to sustain the existing social order by reducing its readers to a kind of wormy mulch of envy, despair and class hatred. But come the revolution, I can tell you this: there's going to be a lot of flying glass.

☙

About this time last year, a friend accused me of having 'let myself go'. And I remember being quite taken aback. I put down the bottle of salad cream I was drinking, and changed the receiver to the other hand, while considering how to reply. 'But my boyfriend says I'm lovely,' I protested, at last. 'He likes me the way I am.' 'Oh, come on,' was the rejoinder. 'Surely you can see he's just saying that.' I bit my lip, slid down in the chair and unbuttoned the waistband on my elasticated jumbo-sized trousers.

Luckily the boyfriend returned at that moment from the chip shop, so I was obliged to ring off. But later, while licking tomato ketchup off the hem of my baggy T-shirt, I told him about the conversation, and asked him what he thought. He said my friend was probably just jealous, and that I should take no notice. But for some reason this cure-all answer failed to satisfy. After all, she was right: I had stopped buying nice clothes, had become addicted to chocolate milk-shakes and taramasalata (sometimes in thrilling combinations), and had started to warm to Shelley Winters as a potential role-model. But what alarmed me most was the memory of my own pathetic little defence: 'My boyfriend says I'm lovely.' I could not believe I had said it.

Leaving aside the attractive jealousy hypothesis for the time being, I told myself that at least the idea of 'letting yourself go' was the wrong phrase, since it belonged to the wrong era. Letting yourself go meant casting aside your boned corset (and having a good scratch), or letting your real eyebrows grow back. You can imagine it in those dour D.H. Lawrence-ish Albert Finney movies ('What about tha' wife?' 'Me wife? Yon bitch uz let hersel' go'). Those were the days when women were deemed to be the human equivalent of the Morning Glory, flowering for about twenty minutes and lucky if someone noticed.

All of this was comforting. But on the other hand, it is undeniable that I let myself get fat and frowzy when I had a boyfriend; and that the minute I became single again I lost weight in butter-mountain proportions and headed for the gym. To anyone familiar with the life story of Elizabeth Taylor this syndrome is a sad cliché, for which I apologize. Prior to cohabitation, I had looked after my body by feeding it occasional salads; but once safely cocooned in coupledom with a man who did a marvellous impression of a priest granting absolution ('Hey, go for it, babycakes; life's too short') I was singing 'Bring out the figgy pudding' from dawn to dusk. This seemed wonderfully liberating until the cold dawn of single life brought me the realization that the only Lonely Hearts advertisements I could answer were the ones that said 'Send photo of flat'.

All of which was how I came to learn about weight-training, and discover my pecs and lats. You wondered where all this was leading, and this is it. Stung by the remark about letting myself go, I decided it was time to pull myself together, which is precisely what weight-training is. You know the way people tune up strings on guitars (dooing-dooing, dung-dung, dang-dang, ding-ding) – well, weight-training is a bit like that, only you have to supply your own sound effects. It is mostly boys who go to my gym, many of them with moustaches, and some of them have even pulled themselves together too tightly.

It is amazing. We have muscles all over the place, some of them happy to respond to attention after about twenty years of disuse. I am particularly fond of the muscles known to us in the weight-training fraternity as 'lats' (the latissimus dorsi) because they pull my shoulders down from where they want to be – viz, around my ears. But I have also discovered some muscles called 'glutes' which are pretty impressive, since I had previously assumed that there resided nothing in this area beyond wibble and wobble.

The jargon is great; I love it. What is a bench press, Auntie Lynne? Well, it is not, as you might think, a huddle in a rugby club changing-room, ho ho. And what do you mean by 'calf extension'? Well, it has nothing to do with veal, ha ha. The nice man with big beach-ball shoulders who taught me to use the machines was impressed that I picked up the terminology with such relish. 'What's next?' he would say, as we finished our warm-ups. 'Quads!' I yelled, like a contestant on a game-show. 'And what do we use for quads?' 'Umm ... the leg press!' I was transported by it all. I remember coming home on the Tube and musing, like Alice in the rabbit-hole, 'Do cats have lats? Do newts have glutes?'

The big issue now is: would I 'let myself go' if a man said to me, 'Listen, two buckets of potato salad won't be the end of the world'? I honestly could not say. Rather cunningly, I did ask the man with the beach-ball shoulders if he would like to go out for a drink, but it turned out he was married already, which was a crying shame. I had fancied the idea of going dancing with him, and wiggling our lats at one another across a crowded room. Friends said we would not have had much to talk about, but I didn't care. What a perfect solution to the man-or-muscle dilemma, I thought. I mean, what an ideal chap for keeping a woman on the straight and narrow.

Somewhere along the line, I got the wrong idea about snails. Influenced by my fondness for Brian in *The Magic Roundabout*, I thought of snails as rather larky characters wearing comical hats and mufflers who deliver wry put-downs. I know this is silly, but you can't legislate for the power of *The Magic Roundabout* over a young person's imagination; and if I grew up expecting sarcasm from molluscs, at least I know where I got the idea. Brian also had a jaunty manner of locomotion, as I recall: reversing back and forth continually, as though engaged in a compulsive seven-point turn. So I rather got the impression that – what with the put-downs and the skidding about – snails were the Bruce Forsyths of the natural world.

So it was a bit of a shock to discover, when I finally took responsibility for a garden, that snails are in fact rather stupid organisms that mechanically chomp through marigolds and delphiniums, and are so blindly partial to a drop of Theakston's Old Peculiar that they can actually be lured into drowning in it. Brian's razor-sharp wit and lightness of foot were clearly unrepresentative of his gastropod friends in general. 'Where be your gibes now?' I say, as I gruesomely pile dead snails and empty shells into a sort of garden-path Golgotha (*pour encourager les autres*). 'Your gambols? Your songs? Your flashes of merriment that were apt to set – er, Dougal and Zebedee in a roar?'

Dealing with pests is one of those problems that women prefer not to face alone. In fact, when discussing separation, I have known women suddenly struck by the thought 'but who would dispose of the spiders?' decide on the instant that the calling-off must be called off. It is sad but true that when a man is around, one automatically crouches on top of a wardrobe saying 'Eek' while the chap does the business with the coal shovel. It all happens so quickly, you see, that you don't have time to explore the sexual politics. 'Cat's got a frog!' you shout, and before you know it the man has taken charge, and you are scaling the curtains.

I have never actually asked a man outright if he is any good with worms, but it is only a matter of time. There we will be: him, me, moonlight, the heady scent of honeysuckle, the flesh trembling, pushing towards the overwhelming question, and I shall have to spoil it by mentioning worms. The funny thing is, of course, that when no spouse is present to stride manfully worm-wards with a piece of cardboard ('Don't worry your head, little missy, I think Mister Worm and I understand one another'), a lone woman simply does it herself. She looks up, sees a worm, thinks 'Why do cats catch *worms*? What do they think it *proves*?' and then rolls it on to a copy of Hello! and flings it back on the garden.

Up until this year, you see, I let the man deal with the snails. 'Ugh,' I said, as I watched him pick them up, 'I couldn't do that. No. no. I couldn't do that.' The idea of handling snails gave me the same species of ab-dabs as the thought of being encased in polystyrene, or forced to listen to a thirty-minute concerto for fingernail and blackboard. Watching my brave chap pulling the little suckers off the pots and plants and hurling them over the wall into an overgrown garden next door (with an encouraging shout of 'Wheee!') I would huddle in the doorway and gaze admiringly at his prowess, all the while thinking that, left to me, the garden would solely comprise tall, bare, ravaged stalks and enormous, menacing, over-stuffed molluscs blocking the path to the shed.

But in fact, of course, I kill them. I don't shout 'Wheee'

and lob them over the wall; I patrol the garden with a special killing-bucket and a pair of tongs, making evil 'snap-snap' noises and cooing 'Daddy's home.' I used to think all creatures were petals in God's daisy-chain – but that was before I joined the Marigold Liberation Army, and learned not to feel compassion. After a successful snail-raid, I even add insult to injury by watching my favourite piece of archive footage from *Nationwide* (shown last year in BBC2's extravaganza *The Lime Grove Story*) where a huge snail called Boozy is shown supping the froth off a pint before suddenly falling off stone dead with a thump. It makes me laugh every time.

I could never love a snail. The great crime writer Patricia Highsmith kept snails, I believe, at her home in Switzerland, but I am not sure this is evidence of affection. She once wrote a terrifying short story in which a foolhardy zoology professor encounters gigantic snails on a remote island, and has his shoulder bitten clean off (munch, munch) by a snail in search of fresh protein. It wasn't funny, but it helped to get the enemy in perspective. I mean, I think she was saying they'd kill us if they had the chance.

Patricia Highsmith was probably intrigued by their homicidal tendencies, and took the more dangerous specimens into town for a pub-crawl, to see how they'd act with a few beers inside them. At which point – of course! – they'd probably put on the hats and mufflers and start saying, 'Nice to see you, to see you nice' while zig-zagging across the bar in the snails' equivalent of the hokey-cokey. I never realized it before. All that skidding about and sarcasm that Brian used to do – perhaps he was simply tiddly.

⁂

I once heard a very scary story concerning a man who lived alone. I sometimes remember it late at night, and get so nervous that I chew the edge of the duvet. Invited to a friend's house for dinner, it seems, this man behaved in a perfectly normal, outgoing manner until the moment attention turned to the serving of Brussels sprouts – when he suddenly got strangely serious.

'One, two, three,' he said to himself, as he carefully ladled the steaming veggies onto his plate. 'Ha ha, oh yes. Four, five, six, *seven*.' The hosts swapped glances, and shifted uncomfortably in their seats. 'More sprouts, John?' asked the hostess, after a pause. At which their guest made a loud scoffing noise and stood up, violently pushing back his chair so that it rucked up the carpet. 'Look,' he said. 'I've got seven sprouts. And forgive me for having two strong sturdy legs to stand on, but seven sprouts is the number of sprouts I *have*.'

No doubt there are many married people, too, who have strong feelings on the subject of sprouts. One recalls those famous cases of men murdering their wives (and getting off with a light fine and a reprimand) for serving up the incorrect number of roasties, or putting the cruet on the wrong place-mat. But it is sitting alone in the evening, I am sure, that encourages crankiness: start out with a harmless little tendency towards obsessive-compulsive behaviour, and within a few months of single life you are not only talking to the characters in *Brookside* but also getting dogmatic about vegetable-consumption and forming advanced crackpot theories on the nature of evil. Since nobody contradicts you (and the goldfish doesn't care) you easily convince yourself that you are 'on the right lines'.

Take the chap I met recently in a Pasadena cake shop. He seemed normal enough: just a bit over-keen for a chat. But then he mentioned that during his solitary hours he had given a lot of thought to the identity of the Antichrist, and had finally settled conclusively on Richard Branson. Everything pointed to it, he said. There's none so blind as those who will not see, etcetera. I thought he was joking, but it gradually dawned on me that he wasn't, and that moreover he was positioned between me and the door.

'Set in your ways' – that's what they call it when single people start getting things out of proportion. 'Don't get set in your ways.' It means: don't use a protractor when setting the coffee table at an angle to the wall; don't attach so much importance to changing the date on your kitchen calendar that you scoot home from work mid-morning to check you've done it. The image conjured up is of a stupid-looking prehistoric animal sinking in mud and muttering, 'Actually, I always buy the *Radio Times* on a *Wednesday*' and 'I asked for kitchen towel, and she bought me *yellow*.'

One need only spend half an hour in a supermarket to see where 'getting set in your ways' can ultimately lead. There is a strange urban myth which says that in supermarkets single people strike up impromptu chats over the rindless streaky in the hope of finding a potential mate. In reality, however, they are more likely to start the conversation because rindless streaky has been occupying their thoughts in the evenings.

The trouble, of course, is to recognize when one's own reasonable preferences and quaint pet theories (attained through a painstaking process of trial and error) turn into pig-headed fixed ideas, or even dangerous obsessions. At what point does it 'get out of hand'? I have a nasty suspicion that it is a phenomenon you can never observe in your own behaviour – one of those clever irregular verbs:

I have rules about things;

You are set in your ways;

He thinks Richard Branson is the Antichrist.

I am assuming, I suppose, that a sane live-in partner prevents the escalation of this behaviour – rather as he might helpfully point out that your clothes are thick with cat-hair or that there is toothpaste up your nostrils. But is it worth taking on a live-in partner just for this function? I can't believe it is. Perhaps, instead, there ought to be some tall, supernatural protector for single people (along the lines of Superman) who could spot a burgeoning obsession with his X-ray vision and wooosh into our homes (with a fanfare) to prevent it from getting a grip.

Thus, just as you were preparing your solitary dinner and thinking 'I don't know. Eight sprouts seems too many, yet six sprouts seems too few,' he would suddenly appear at your side and dash the whole bag to the ground, releasing you from their terrible influence. 'A close call,' he twinkles (with arms akimbo and a smile reminiscent of Richard Branson's). 'Lumme,' you say, 'was I really counting *sprouts*?' 'It's all over now,' he chuckles, patting you on the shoulder. 'Just don't let it happen again, you hear?'

And as he turns horizontal and flies off through the kitchen door with a cheery salute, you slide down the wall to a sitting position and think – with ample justification – 'I wonder if I'm spending too much time on my own?'

⌒

Years ago, I was privileged to meet one of the men who first applied the word 'vector' to a type of bank account. I met him at an historic moment, actually, because he had just emerged from the selfsame shirtsleeve-and-braces design consultancy think-tank meeting at which the full kennel-name of Vector ('Indigo Vector') had been finally settled upon. He looked tired but happy – like a miner, perhaps, at the end of a 12-hour shift, or a brain surgeon who had just achieved a complicated transplant.

Of course, the proceedings of this meeting were not disclosed, but from his exhausted but triumphant state I somehow deduced it had resembled the jury room in Sidney Lumet's *Twelve Angry Men* – you know, sweaty, tense, touch-

and-go, life-in-the-balance. Perhaps opposition to 'Indigo Vector' had been fierce; the 'Blue Streak' lobby was unshiftable. I imagined my chap taking the righteous white-suited Henry Fonda role, quietly fighting his colleagues every inch of the way, and remaining cool while his enemies dabbed their brows with big hankies.

Had I never met him at all, however, I would have imagined something quite different. I would have assumed that the naming of a new bank account must be a work of inspiration, and that, as such, it must come from a humble individual sitting alone in a padded cell – rather in the manner of the contract Hollywood writer under the old studio system. We could call him Mankowitz. 'Get Mankowitz on to this!' the board would command. And a secretary would place a sheet of paper in Mankowitz's in-tray, describing the new bank account and expecting a result by noon.

Mankowitz would come in at ten, take off his hat, shuffle the papers without removing the long cigarette between his fingers, and then start to type short one-liners, stopping occasionally only to pinch the bridge of his nose under his wire-rimmed specs.

Indigo Vector.
The bank that likes to say yes.
I want to be a tomato.
For the little things in life.
They're tasty, tasty, very very tasty, they're very tasty.
Once bitten, forever smitten.
We won't make a drama out of a crisis.

And then at half past ten, he would stop for coffee.

Perhaps I harbour too strong an attachment to romantic notions of solitary genius. Perhaps I have too little respect for the massed talents of the advertising industry. But somehow

I prefer the Mankowitz option. The idea of a gaggle of blokes in expensive whistles sitting together and running the paltry word Vector up a flag-pole fills me with a strange and yawning sadness.

I remembered all this because I have recently discovered the surreal world of paint colour names (Comet, Murmur, Quiescence, Evensong, Early December) and I simply cannot bear to believe that these were chosen by a committee in a designer boardroom. There is too much poetry involved, too much imaginative intimacy.

'Right, then,' I said, at the paint counter. 'I'll have a litre of Hazy Downs please, with Tinker for the skirting,' and I caught my breath at hearing the words. It was as though the spirit of a mad poet had breezed through. Walls of hazy downs; and 'Tinker' for the skirting. Wow.

Just look at a strip of green Dulux shades – 'Spring dance, April coppice, Verge, Racecourse, Meadow land, Treetop' – and you can see this poet, can't you, his eyes closed, straining to hear birdsong in the rustling trees outside his cell window. 'More greens,' he smiles to himself, momentarily forgetting the shackles that bind him to the damp stone walls. And he falls into a trance. 'Curly kale,' he intones, relishing the shapes it makes in his mouth. 'Shady fern, Mystic moon, Fresh breeze, Elderwater, Trickle.'

'What was the last one?' snaps the man from Dulux who is taking this down. 'Trickle,' he repeats.

What I am building up to is a confession. I keep meeting people who think I write this column in a darkened room in a small flat, with just cats for company, and that I write it all myself out of my very own brain. Whereas of course this is a mere illusion, and in fact the writing of this column is a well-organized team affair involving a large number of hacks in consultancy roles, a weekly meeting (with minutes), and an all-day creative thrash-out, in which each person writes a paragraph and then the whole thing is put together by a complicated voting procedure. I mean 'Single Life'? You must be joking. There are loads of us here. Loads. You should see the washing-up.

I am sorry to ruin the illusion, but we all have to learn some time that there is no Mankowitz in the advertising industry; there is no mad poet dreaming of Dulux colours; it's all done by meetings. 'Now, a few more greens and thank goodness we can stop for lunch. Anybody got a word that goes with Kale? Anybody?' 'Er ... "yard", sir.' 'Mmm, so you think we should call it "Yard kale", Robbins? Sounds all right to me.' 'No, sir. I meant – er, kaleyard.' 'Oh.' 'There's something called curly kale in the dictionary, sir.' 'Splendid. All right, hands up for Curly kale. Next!'

⁀

I have never lingered in cosmetics halls. In fact, I have never really understood what they are for. Why do they invariably lurk at the entrance of department stores, blocking one's progress to the real business inside? Is it a subtle fumigation process? Or is the idea to soften you up? The luxuriant chrome and lights, the shrill exciting perfumes, the gallons of moisturizer (in tiny pots) – I figure that this sensual riot is designed to trip up the women, and remind them that shopping is basically self-flattery and treats. By the time you actually buy something, you see, you feel so madly feminine that you shell out wildly for an extra tube of bath sealant.

But I am only guessing, because personally I always draw a deep breath at the threshold to the shop, take a last memorizing look at my list ('Draino; Cat-flap accessories; Something for getting Ribena stains out of sofa') and then whiffle quickly and invisibly between the little counters, tacking athwart this alien sea of feminine trinketry with my eyes half-closed against the unaccustomed glamour of it all. If I pause nervously to examine a lipstick, and a lady asks 'Can I help you?' I freeze, and then scuttle sharpish to the lifts.

But suddenly, a few weeks ago, I felt an urge to paint my fingernails. It was weird and unaccountable. One minute I was quite normal and stable, attempting to play a well-regulated game of hide and seek with cats who can't (or won't) count to twenty. And the next, I was overtaken by an access of femininity, humming 'I Enjoy Being a Girl' with brio, and breezing into cosmetics halls demanding a range of nail colours and offering to trade unwanted cat-flap accessories by way of payment. Funny how life can change.

Single life suddenly looked quite different, you see: I caught a glimpse of another world, originating in the sort of TV advertisement where pink gauze curtains billow sensuously in a boudoir full of white light and a woman with fantastic hair pampers herself with a beauty product (or tampons). Most people probably regard nail varnish as either functional or tacky, but to me it acquired the force of revelation. Previously the idea of pampering myself meant watching the *EastEnders* omnibus when I had already seen both episodes in the week. But now it meant inhabiting an aura of solitary voluptuousness, spending whole yummy evenings watching paint dry.

Now, the interesting thing about nail polish is that it comes without instructions. Did you know this? This was my first setback, really, and it was one from which I never properly recovered. The other interesting thing is that nail polish remover, if you splash it about too liberally, removes polish quite indiscriminately – from your best sandals, for example, and your chest of drawers. Also, it is not a good idea to put used cotton buds, soaked with nail polish remover, directly on a mahogany dining table, because not only does the surface mysteriously acquire pits and scars, but the lacerations have white hair growing out of them, which won't come off again, ever.

Within minutes of starting my new regime, I had run up damages to an approximate replacement value of twelve hundred pounds. But I was not down-hearted. I had applied a transparent goo of base-coat to all of my fingernails (including the right-hand ones, which were tricky) and was now ready to drink sherbet, eat Turkish delight, and watch an American mini-series until the next stage. 'I'm strictly a female female,' I sang, 'Da da dum di da Dum de dee.' I picked up the remote control from the carpet and was surprised to discover that a layer of speckled gunk had attached itself to all the nails that had come in contact with the floor. Spit. Peering at the other hand (which looked OK), I cautiously tapped all the nails with a finger to check they were dry. They weren't.

Three hours later my fifth attempt at a base-coat was almost dry, but I was feeling strangely detached from my surroundings, because I had just spent a whole evening not using my fingers. Every impulse to pick up a tissue, or stroke the cat, or wipe hair from my eyes had been followed once (with disastrous results) and thereafter strenuously denied. At one point, the phone had rung, and after a period of whimpering with indecision I had answered it by picking up the receiver between my elbows and then dropping it on the desk, in a manner reminiscent of thriller heroines tied to kitchen chairs. 'Hello?' it said faintly from the desktop. 'Help!' I yelled, kneeling beside the receiver, and waggling my fingers like a madwoman. 'Hello?' it said again, and went dead.

Eventually I took the whole lot off again, partly because the removal process was the only one I was good at, partly because I realized that novice nail-painting is not something to be attempted alone, after all. It requires the attendance of slaves. I did a swift impression of Lady Macbeth (damned spot, and all that), and went to bed. And there I dreamed of waltzing through bright cosmetics halls, dressed in pink gauze, carrying bags and bags of lovely self-indulgent stuff for getting Ribena stains out of the sofa.

~

First, there is something I should explain: in May 1968, when the world stage resounded to the lobbing of cobbles in the streets of Paris, I recorded in my personal diary the purchase of a maroon skirt. I make no apology. To me, you see, at twelve years old, this was an *événement*. Maroon wool, slightly too big, zip at the front, I was proud. Moreover, conscious of the heavy responsibility owed by all diarists to future historians, I thoughtfully taped the price label to the page. 'Etam,' it says, '£sd: 19/11'. I still have it (the label, not the skirt). It is before me now.

In the intervening years, I have of course laughed at the schoolgirl hubris – fancy preserving an Etam label; did I imagine that the wild-eyed time-capsule people would wrest it from my grasp and bury it along with a copy of the Maastricht treaty for unborn post-nuclear generations to gape and wonder at? Ha ha ha. But now something has happened. The University of Reading has acquired a 'Centre for Ephemera Studies', dedicated to the preservation of can labels, leaflets, and all such throwaway stuff. Good grief, my Etam label – someone really wants it. It is like waking up in the cold light of a science fiction novel. Well, do it to Julia, that's what I say.

Personally, I wouldn't want to be the University of Reading at the moment. Leaving aside the obvious horror entailed in suddenly finding oneself transmogrified into a red-brick academic institution in the middle of nowhere, tons of old shed-clearings must daily be screeching through the gates by special courier. 'More bus tickets from well-wishers,' says the dumper truck driver, as he cheerfully pulls his lever and sends several hundredweight of brown-paper parcels slither-ing down in a heap. The remit of the centre is to preserve only printed matter, but the chronic hoarders of carpet off-cuts will be much too excited to notice. 'People throw these bits away, with no sense of heritage, but we have kept these sacks of Cyril Lord for thirty years,' says the covering letter. 'Please don't try returning it to us, we have moved. We hope you find much interest also in the tins of paint.'

But if the university sinks under the weight of empty seed packets and Brillo boxes, it will only serve them right. What a terrible idea, to confer academic respectability on the worst of human failings. Besides, since we feel guilt about having a throwaway culture, for God's sake let's have the exhilaration too. *Chuck it right away, Kay; sling it in the bin, Vin; take it to the tip, Pip; dump it in the sea, Lee. There must be fifty ways to lose a label.* Who cares if the 'details of our everyday life' are not remem-bered for ever? Who do we think we are? This sort of vanity is all right when you are twelve, but let's snap out of this worship of the design-classic Coke bottle, before it is too late.

It used to be the case that cultural artefacts of all sorts – not just H.P. Sauce labels – were consigned to the dustbin. And it was better, healthier, that way. The old made way for the new. Television programmes were shown, then wiped; films were distributed once; records were released, sold, deleted; nice old buildings were wantonly knocked down; and a collection of old cinema tickets was something that alarmingly dropped out of a shoebox in front of guests, making you flush red, grab your purse, and run away to Sweden. But now the culture has been telescoped, which is why it's hard to remember what year it is, and why shopping in the Virgin Megastore is such a depressing experience. When a person can still buy Monkees albums in 1993, it reduces her faith in the natural workings of progress.

So here is a rallying call. Let us face forward, dump some

big ones, and move on. It needs no ghost of Sigmund Freud to point out that the new discipline of ephemera studies represents anal retention on a vast, global and terrifying scale. Besides, if we carry on like this, there will be no future historians to thank us for the postcard, so it's all a vainglorious waste of time in any case. By the year 2000, if we are not all dead through millennial terror, economic incompetence, or holy war, I confidently predict we will have disappeared under inundations of books and videos and lovingly preserved Etam labels.

⌒

I swore off caviare on Sunday night. The cats took it badly, but I stood firm, and told them they would thank me in the end. Having watched an hour-long Channel 4 documentary about the polluted River Volga and its toxic sturgeon, I sadly added caviare to my mental list of proscribed foods, finding surprisingly little comfort in the thought that I never eat it anyway. According to a current crack-'em-up joke among the Volga fishermen (who admittedly rejoice in a very peculiar sense of humour), even the Kremlin bureaucrats no longer dare to eat the stuff, so I was not over-reacting. Industrial pollutants and agricultural pesticides are poisoning the river to a point where the giant beluga no longer swims gaily in its waters but is reduced to a big stuffed ugly fish in a museum, dusted weekly by a woman in a scarf.

Given that caviare is not a staple food (and that you have to eat quite a lot of it to feel any ill effects), the programme wasn't exactly alarmist, and I wasn't exactly alarmed. But my heart sank as I recognized the beginnings of a new idée fixe. The trouble with food scares is that only rarely are they called off; a warning siren wails out the danger, but there is no equivalent to the All Clear. This means that susceptible, obedient people with no minds of their own (like me) still pick up little trays of Welsh lamb in supermarkets and then put them back down again, just wondering in a vague, confused kind of way whether the effect of Chernobyl will wear off in their lifetimes. It is possible to get stuck.

Personally I don't buy French apples (why, I don't remember); I don't buy cat-food marked 'beef' (mad cat disease); and I am wary of eggs (Mrs Currie). Making meals is therefore quite difficult, as you can imagine. In fact, if there is ever a scare involving big economy sacks of Maltesers, quite frankly I am done for.

This is mainly a personality failing, obviously. If nobody says stop, I carry on. I reckon I am one of the very few people alive today who understand why a Japanese soldier would still be fighting the Second World War. A couple of years ago I was obliged to forgo my visits to a very pleasant supervised gym just because every time I was given a repetitive exercise ('Breathe out and pull; breathe in, relax; out and pull, and in, relax') I found I would obediently repeat it until the tutor checked up on me, *regardless of the interval*. 'Done ten of those yet?' he would enquire, in a kindly tone. 'Fifty-six,' I would blurt out, red-faced. I finally gave it up when I realized that he might one day set me going on an exercise and then pop out to post a letter and be run down by a furniture van. In which case I would be left to row an imaginary skiff for the rest of my natural life.

The idea about food scares, presumably, is that you use your own judgement, but without information I don't understand how it's done. A fortnight after Chernobyl, do you just decide not to dwell on the nasty idea that contamination lasts thousands of years (or whatever), and choose to make a traditional shepherd's pie – even if it cooks itself without help and out-shines the candlelight on the dining table? 'Life's too short,' you reason (quite aptly, in the circumstances). But isn't salmonella still rife in the chicken coops, aren't cattle still waltzing in the pens? They are probably doing a full-scale mazurka by now.

On the caviare front there is less to worry about, obviously. 'I hope there's no caviare in this,' is not something the average attentive cat-owner thinks to herself when doling out the Whiskas. On the other hand, the chances of us hearing that the Volga has been cleaned up (even if it happens) are remarkably slim, so the old Japanese soldier syndrome takes over once again, I'm afraid. 'Don't eat the prawns,' Julie Walters once hissed alarmingly in a Victoria Wood sketch. 'They tread water at sewage outlets with their mouths open.' Likewise, from now on I shall raise a skinny warning hand at people in the act of eating caviare canapés, and remind them of the latest unfunny sturgeon jokes from the fisherfolk of the Volga. Either that, of course, or only respond to invitations that promise '6pm–9pm, Cocktails and Maltesers'.

⌒

According to the first-hand reports, what tends to happen is this. You are lying in a hospital bed, approaching death, and then suddenly you lift out of your body and look down on yourself. This is weird enough to start with, of course; but before your rationality can fully take stock – 'That's very odd, me on the ceiling, I expect it was the toasted cheese' – you are propelled, helpless and at great velocity, along a dark tunnel towards a wonderful welcoming light. No thought of passport, hand-baggage or travellers' cheques detains you; nor do you slap your hand to your brow with the cry 'Oh no, I left the iron on.' Instead, you emerge into a beautiful, timeless, tranquil garden where you feel blissfully happy, and decide to stay for eternity, if not *weeks*.

Of course you are also dragged away again. Suddenly, with a dreadful finality, you are dropped back in your body, and it's all over, your vision is fled, you are condemned to life. But you are never the same again. Possibly your experience confirms the notion of life after death, possibly it proves only that imagination is the last thing to go. Whichever way you see it, you have been blessed.

Personally, I have always yearned for an out-of-body-experience. (With a body like mine, so would you.) My only fear was that my idea of paradise is so cheap and materialistic that my tunnel would end, not in the tranquillity of Elysian fields, nor beside still waters, but in a celestial shopping arcade (modelled on Bentalls of Kingston), from which I would return with beany hats and specially printed souvenirs: 'My sister went to Heaven and all she got me was this lousy T-shirt.' This sense of personal unworthiness, however, only increases one's awe at the genuine wonderful thing, and on Sunday I watched BBC1's *Everyman* programme about near-death experiences with big round eyes and my mouth open. Even if you don't believe in Heaven, you can believe in the near-death experience. These people had seen something. They thought it was lovely. It was thirteen years since one woman's privileged return from the undiscovered country, yet she still had light in her eyes when she spoke about it. In earlier times, these people would have been revered as saints, I thought.

The only puzzle was why nobody mentioned Lewis Carroll. Tunnel, garden, I don't know, it rings bells. What *was* mentioned, however, was a miserable wet-blanket scientific theory which suggested in no uncertain terms that the near-death experience is a mere perceptual illusion – something that happens inside the brain when your resistance is low – and that in reality you don't go anywhere, not even Bentalls, you just think you do. This was a shock, especially since it sounded so plausible. Dr Susan Blackmore, a cheerful academic with a no-nonsense approach and a leaning towards Buddhism, has been researching the phenomenon for years, and what she said, basically, was that your inhibitory cells stop firing, causing masses of excitation. I felt terrible. I sat down. So it was really true, what they told me. There is no shopping after death.

'What happened to you back there? We thought we'd lost you!'

'Oh, it was just some uncontrolled firing in the temporal lobe, silly! The accompanying rush of endorphins (peptide neurotransmitters) just persuaded me I was having a frightfully good time when in fact I wasn't.'

'Oh. So it wasn't like Heaven, then?'

'Well, in a way it was. I mean, I wore a blue frock and had a pony, which was nice, and there was a treacle well and a pile of comics, but it didn't mean anything. It was just that my brain had lost its grip on the normal model of reality, and had constructed one from memory and imagination, rather than from the evidence of the senses.'

I suppose the near-death experience never did prove the existence of the immortal soul, but I have to admit I sneakingly thought it did. But that's all in the past now. What saddens me equally is the thought that if the near-death experience is an illusion, there is no near-life experience either, which leaves a big question-mark hanging over the glassy-eyed travellers of the London Underground. Previously I had supposed they were dead people on spiritual awayday tickets, investigating the joys of the other side. But if they aren't, then who the hell *are* they?

The Only Event of Any Importance
That Ever Happened to Me

I got stuck in the lift last week. I had been working a bit late, and the lift was waiting innocently at the right floor, so – fool that I was – I thought I'd travel down in it and save on the wear and tear to the support hosiery. The doors closed pretty efficiently, but then nothing else would work: the doors wouldn't open again, and the lift wouldn't move. I told myself to breathe deeply, and not panic. Funnily enough, that didn't work either. The whole of Hancock's *The Lift* flashed before my eyes.

I knew I stood a good chance of being rescued, since several people were still dittling about, pretending to be working. Nevertheless I was quite frightened, especially as they didn't seem able to hear my knocking and calling ... or my BANGING and SHOUTING ... or even my POUNDING and SCREAMING. There was a glass panel in the door, and I could see people wandering soundlessly between rooms, totally oblivious to my plight. Had premature burial come to the Old Marylebone Road?

Even when at last I managed to attract someone's attention, the relief was short-lived, since it was soon discovered that the door wouldn't open from the outside either. Besides, it turned out that my so-called rescuer had watched Billy Wilder's film *Ace in the Hole* on television the night before, and was immediately struck by the parallel. Shouting through six inches of metal, she assured me that I would be perfectly all right, of course, but that they might need to drill down from the top. 'We'll have you out of there in no time,' she said. 'Three weeks at the outside.'

Gradually the alarm went out, and people gathered around the lift to see me in my vertical coffin. Having endured many a Roger Corman movie in my youth, I knew the proper Ligeia drill, but I decided against breaking my fingernails tearing at the glass for their benefit. Instead I behaved impeccably, shrugging and smiling, and waving cheery hellos to the succession of familiar faces who took it in turns to peer solemnly in at me. It was like one of those reconstructions of a baby's-eye view of childbirth: big faces with impersonal expressions looking in and mouthing stuff like, 'She's in there, sure enough. But how are we going to get her out?'

In the end, our fast-thinking Chief Sub ran and located some sort of lift-key which, when properly applied to the door, alarmed him by sending me plummeting down (inside the lift) to freedom.

There is only one interesting aspect to this no-doubt commonplace experience. It is that throughout the whole terrifying ordeal, I seemed to hear the voice of the Lord. And he said to me, 'Here you are then, Lynne. Here's your *Margins* for next week. Don't say I never give you anything.'

⌒

To celebrate the 3,000th *Listener* crossword, I thought I might share a little secret with you. Shout it aloud in Gath and Hebron: nobody on the *Listener* staff has the first idea of how to do the *Listener* crossword. For years, we have been convinced that the clues are actually coded messages from MI5.

Speaking personally, it's not only crosswords that I can't do.

All sorts of brain teasers leave my brain completely unexcited. The ones I particularly dislike are those that are designed to develop your verbal reasoning skills, where you are supposed to infer a whole system of relationships from a few key bits of information. For example: a) 'Julie has a dog but it does not have blue eyes'; b) 'John knows all the words to *Melancholy Baby* but can't quite get the tune'; c) 'Sylvester only recognizes words with fewer than *four letters*'; d) 'The dog will sing, but only for *Maltesers*'.

Perhaps my dislike for these exercises explains why I found it so hard to get started on Iris Murdoch's novel, *The Book and the Brotherhood*. She launches straight into this kind of information about a vast number of characters (Conrad is taller than Gulliver, though Gulliver is considered tall; Gerard is Tamar's uncle but Violet's cousin; Gerard, Jenkin and Duncan all wear dinner-jackets), with nary a thought for those of us hastily sketching diagrams on the fly-leaf.

So which puzzles *can* I do? Well, I will confess that I have a certain aptitude – given the right airport-lounge – for the ones that present you with a block of letters, and ask you to find the hidden words.

```
W A R I S T O T L E
I K Z P D F R J Z P
T R A C T A T U S S
T Y F R J Z P M D T
G X Z O L V T K J S
E M P I R I C A L O
N S F R E C T N O C
S V H A S O N T E R
T N E B T X O E T A
E A G I Z Y A R L T
I B E E P E X T J E
N C L V H O B B E S
```

Now, to the untrained eye, this looks like a mere mess of jumbled letters. But I think I can demonstrate something pretty startling.

```
W A R I S T O T L E
I K Z P D F R J Z P
T R A C T A T U S S
T Y F R J Z P M D T
G X Z O L V T K J S
E M P I R I C A L O
N S F R E C T N O C
S V H A S O N T E R
T N E B T X O E T A
E A G I Z Y A R L T
I B E E P E X T J E
N C L V H O B B E S
```

Reflections on Culture

Since the book is now out, it is too late to ask Susan Hill to be gentle with me. As from yesterday, a surging modern sequel to Daphne du Maurier's *Rebecca* has crashed and boiled by moonlight into the bookshops, and my name – Mrs de Winter – is once again in common parlance, along with Rebecca and Mrs Danvers, and Mad Ben the beachcomber. ('No shell here,' nods gap-toothed Ben mysteriously in my dreams at night. 'Been diggin' since forenoon. No shell here.')

Ho hum. Crash. Boil. That's the trouble with being shy and mousy. When you are the sort of nervous person who pushes the shards of a broken ornament to the back of a drawer so that the servants don't find out ('Oh lord, that's one of our treasures, isn't it?' quips your husband, helpfully), it is natural that people should go right ahead and publish sequels about you, without bothering to ask you first. In my worst moments I think Mrs Danvers was right, I should have chucked myself out of an upstairs window and done everyone a favour. But the trouble with being *Rebecca*'s nameless heroine is this: supposing Susan Hill had taken me out for a coastal drive and then explained, 'I'm asking you to be in my new novel, you little fool!' – well, I would have had no option but to swoon my acceptance, wouldn't I?

But I have changed a lot since *Rebecca*, since those ashes blew towards us with the salt wind from the sea. And I just hope Susan Hill is aware of it. The fact is, I experienced a quite surprising character change just at the point when Daphne du Maurier's narrative left us – Maxim and me – on that mad, desperate nocturnal drive westwards towards the blazing Manderley. You may remember the scene. I spotted the giveaway glow on the horizon, and suggested, feebly, that it was the northern lights. 'That's not the northern lights,' said hubby, all grim and lantern-jawed (as usual). 'That's Manderley.' And he put his foot down. 'Maxim,' I whined. 'Maxim, what is it?' But he didn't answer, just drove faster, much faster. I felt cold, very cold. It was dark, horribly dark. The sky above our heads was inky black. But the sky on the horizon was not dark at all. It was shot with crimson, like a splash of blood. 'It's the bloody house!' I yelled, suddenly. 'That snotty cow in the black frock has set fire to the bloody house!'

Well, you can imagine the consternation. We came off the road. The car juddered to a halt. There was a hiss of steam. The ash still blew towards us with the salt winds of the sea, but I beat it off my jacket saying, 'Ugh! Ash! Yucky! Look!' Maxim could not believe his ears. 'Stop it, you idiot!' he said, but it was the wrong thing to say. 'And you can stop calling me an idiot as well!' I said, and socked him on the jaw. It was terribly peculiar; not like me at all. The author watched in stunned amazement, and then asked very quietly whether she could have a word.

The whole point of *Rebecca*, she explained patiently, was that I – as the modest, hapless, mooncalf heroine – should serve as a role-model for readers yet unborn, as the acceptable face of womanhood. Surely I could see that? 'First we have Rebecca,' she said; 'she's sexy and manipulative and selfish. You see? Then we've got Mrs Danvers, who is dark and jealous and self-sacrificing and is obviously everybody's mother because she knows their faults and judges by impossible standards and rests her chin on their shoulder. And then there's you, the victim. And you haven't got a clue, basically. But because you are well intentioned, not very bright, motivated by gratitude and love, and terrorized by a fear of failure, you're the heroine. Everyone loves you! Trust me! You are a great modern archetype! One day your followers will include the Princess of Wales!'

But I couldn't help thinking, 'Where's the fun in that?' So I divorced Maxim, took half the insurance money on Manderley, learnt to sail, wrote a book on sexual politics, broke a lot of ornaments and felt much better. That's all there is, I think. Except that I decided to call myself Jackie. It comes as a surprise to some people, but as I always say, it's a great deal better than nothing.

❧

Sometimes, in the middle of the night, I wake up in my little flat, turn on the light, and burst into tears with relief. 'Oh kitties,' I gasp. 'What a terrible dream! I dreamed I was in the Algarve on holiday on my own again!' The awoken cats (God bless them) at first assume an air of polite concern. But at the word 'Algarve', they exchange weary glances (the feline equivalent of 'Tsk') and settle their heads back down on their paws. My buried-alive-in-Portugal saga seems to have lost its news value.

Meanwhile, I witter on. 'I am in this café, you see, and I am reading the phrase-book. And all I can say in Portuguese is that I want two coffees, and four teas with milk, and lots of cakes! But I don't really want all these drinks because I'm on my own! And they keep bringing cakes and teas and coffees, and I don't know how to say Stop! and the teas keep coming and it's like the Sorcerer's Apprentice and ...' I look around and see that nobody is listening.

The good thing about this Algarve nightmare is that at least it covers everything you might want to have a nightmare about – from waking up in a box, to doing Finals in Sanskrit, to being drowned in a flash flood of Twinings. It's all there. A friend of mine, who frequently suffers from the Finals dream, says he sometimes manages to double the anxiety by imagining that if he doesn't pass this impossible exam, he won't be allowed to reach the age of thirty-five; he will be obliged to go back to eleven and start again. Yike. In a similar exercise, I sometimes ring the changes on my Algarve nightmare by imagining that while I order the usual never-ending buckets of tea and coffee, I am unaware the laws of the country have been changed, so I am slung into jail for some sort of beverage transgression.

Why am I going on about it? Because I have been studying a little phrase-book I picked up in Italy on my last holiday, and have been rather alarmed by it. *L'Inglese come si parla* has worried me, I admit, ever since I first discovered I had goofed in the shop and bought the wrong sort of phrase-book – intended for Italian visitors to England, rather than the other way around. 'What would you charge to drive me to Richmond?' was the first phrase I saw in it, helpfully spelled out in pretend-phonetics: *Huot uud iu ciaadg tu draiv mi tu Ritc'mond?* And I thought, hang on, this can't be right. Richmond is miles away.

But what I didn't fully appreciate at the time was what a nightmare experience the Italian visitor would have if he allowed this little phrase-book to govern his expectations of England. Because close attention reveals this newly printed publication to have been written either: a) by someone trying to push back the boundaries of existential terror; b) by someone who got all his information from watching Ealing comedies; or c) in 1948.

It's the telltale references to trams that first set you thinking. Then you notice that the pubs close at 10 o'clock, the planes stop at Renfrew, and there are jam omelettes on the bill of fare.

The world is suddenly all Sidney Tafler and black and white. In a tobacconist's shop, the choice of cigarettes is Gold Flake, Players and Capstan; and the lonely Italian visitor in search of a girlfriend proceeds at once to a dance hall. '*Dhis tiun is veri na(i)s, isn't it?*' he says to his partner, peering over her shoulder at the phrase-book, and speaking like a computer. He riffles a few pages. '*Iu aa(r) e wanderful daanser! Mei ai sii iu ho(u)um? Huot is iu(r) adres?*' Encouraged to dabble in less formal English, he tells his new lady-friend she is '*(e) nai(i)s litl bit ov guuz*' (a nice little bit of goods). Something about all this makes me intensely worried on his behalf.

I mean, what would happen if he arrived at Victoria Station, and shouted (as he is advised here), '*Poorter! Te(i)k dhis laghidg tu dhe Braiten trein!*' ('Porter! Take this luggage to the Brighton train'). There would be some sort of riot. Alas, the British public would never guess he was living in some parallel phrase-book universe, would they? They would just assume he was asking for a punch in the eye. 'Wash the car, and give it a good greasing,' he commands at a petrol station. But what's this? Biff! Boff! Ooof! Crawling back to the car, clutching his abdomen in one hand and his phrase-book in the other, he mutters, '*Dhets dhe ghidi limit!*' (That's the giddy limit).

I do wonder whether the book was published in a spirit of mischief by someone obsessed with Ealing films, because actually the story that emerges from its pages is rather like an Ealing plot. Poor guileless foreigner (played by Alec Guinness, perhaps) works hard to overcome loneliness by using authentic popular slang such as 'nose-rag', 'old horse' and 'cheese it!' and nobody knows what the hell he is talking about. '*Dhets ool mai ai end Beti Maarten!*' he exclaims jocularly ('That's all my eye and Betty Martin'), amid general shrugs.

To make matters worse, the phrase 'To pull the plonker' is mysteriously omitted from L'*Inglese come si parla*. So the poor bloke keeps hitting the deck without ever understanding the insistent question on all English people's lips.

⌒

Occasionally, we television critics like to reflect on our lives and pull a few strands together. In particular, we like to emphasize that, far from wasting our childhoods (not to mention adult-hoods) mindlessly gorming at The Virginian and The Avengers, we spent those couch-potato years in rigorous preparation for our chosen career. 'It's been tough,' we reflect thought-fully (as our eyes dart unbeckoned to the nearest flickering screen). 'I mean, er, gosh, Streets of San Francisco, I love this. Oh yes, of course there were a few dodgy moments during the second run of Blankety Blank when I feared I might not make it, that the pace was simply too hard. But I pulled through. And leaving aside the damage to the optic nerve, I can honestly say that watching wall-to-wall drivel was the best – ahem – mental investment I ever made.'

I know, I know. Such pious fraud fools nobody. But in the week that saw the thirty-fifth anniversary of BBC1's Blue Peter, and in which I calculated that I watched this enjoyable, educative programme, girl and woman, for a total of fifteen years, I simply felt obliged to trawl for a valid extenuation. In reality, of course, I watched it because I loved it, because it was live and dangerous, and because the invited animals acted up, refused to eat, and sometimes dragged presenters clear off the set. Most of all, however, I watched for its sugges-tion of that strange made-it-myself domestic world (reached, perhaps, through the airing-cupboard) in which Mummy's work-basket was filled with Fablon off-cuts, while Daddy was a kindly twinkler in carpet slippers who would happily drill a hole in a piece of wood ('Hand it here, youngster!'); you only had to ask.

Some people disliked *Blue Peter* for this cosy middle-class idyll; they got chips on their shoulders. But I thrived on these glimpses of a parallel universe. I adored the fanciful idea of aunties who exclaimed, 'What a lovely present! How ingenious to think of painting an egg-box and making it into a fabulous jewellery case!' Wisely, however, I stayed on the right side of the airing-cupboard, not dabbling in glitter and squeezy bottles; also, I recognized cheap tacky home-made stuff when I saw it, and refused to get involved. Only once in thirty-five glorious *Blue Peter* years did I let slip my guard (oh, woe) and attempt to make 'jelly eggs' as a nice surprise for a family Easter. I regretted it instantly. It was a terrible mistake. One day, they will find 'Jelly Eggs' engraved on my heart, just next to the inexpressibly mournful 'Copy fits, no queries'.

The jelly eggs instructions looked simple enough, but that's no excuse.

1) Take an egg, make a tiny hole in each end, and then just *blow* the contents through the tiny weeny hole, leaving the shell empty.
2) Boil up some jelly.
3) Cover one of the tiny holes with a small piece of sticky tape.
4) Pour the jelly into the shell, then pop it into the fridge, where it will set. Now, just picture the surprise of the adults on Easter morning when they take the top off your egg and find the jelly inside!

Whatever possessed me to try this at home? Could I blow an egg? No, not without blowing my brains out. Would a piece of sticky tape keep the jelly inside (assuming I could pour it into a tiny hole without a funnel)? No, the only thing that worked, finally, was an Elastoplast – the big brick-red fabric sort, generally used for heels. Would the egg-shell mould the jelly into the shape of a perfect egg? No, because the jelly seeped into the Elastoplast overnight, and sank to half-way. Were the adults dumb-struck with surprise when they ate their Easter breakfast? No, because they had all been involved in this disastrous enterprise at some stage or another, urging me in my own interests to see sense and give the whole thing up.

But I never lost my love for *Blue Peter*. I now hear that under pressure from the real world they have sealed up the old airing-cupboard door, which is a shame. *Blue Peter* taught me that when my own turn as auntie came around, I should exclaim, 'That's lovely, how clever, is it a tissue box with my name on it in glitter?' – thus making a little girl quite happy. So it just goes to show. Watching fifteen years' worth of television does teach you something, sometimes.

Alas, I am perplexed again. A few weeks ago, a writer chum phoned me to ask for some help with a difficult ethical question, so naturally I pulled a straight face immediately, rested my fingertips lightly together (tricky when holding a receiver) and suggested she proceed. A friend had left an expensive winter coat in her flat, by mistake, she explained, then flown abroad for six weeks. 'I see,' I said, nodding thoughtfully; 'And so? What?'

My chum's question was this: if I were in her position, *would I wear the coat?*

I was so shocked by the very idea that I instantly abandoned my rational, objective Michael Ignatieff impersonation. 'No,' I said flatly. 'No, I would not.' 'Why?' she asked.

Well, I said, first I would be worried about the safety of the coat, you know, down the shops, bloke on a ladder, tin of paint, Norman Wisdom, ha ha ha. Second, I would be almost suicidally flummoxed in company if anyone remarked: 'Nice coat, where's it from?' But really and honestly, I wouldn't wear it because it wasn't mine.

Now my friend was much taken with this tin-of-paint idea. When she rang other people for further ethical and practical viewpoints, she found that the irrational Fear of Paint not only entered other people's neurotic purview, but could easily be brought to dominate it.

But what she didn't find, apparently, was anyone else who said, 'No, I wouldn't wear it because it isn't mine.' So she wore the coat, recklessly defied the malign god of magnolia gloss, and eventually decided to write a piece for the *Guardian* about the whole damn thing.

And my point (at last) is this. She told me she was writing an article in which I would – nameless, of course – appear. She read me her description of my response, and told me precisely when the piece would be published.

Such careful, respectful and scrupulous behaviour put me to shame. Because when it comes to other people's anecdotes – other people's 'stuff' which might come in handy to illustrate a point in a column or a story – I rip it straight off the hanger without asking, shout 'Yes! This will do nicely!', and publish it in a newspaper. Which is the exact equivalent of wearing it to the open day at the Jackson Pollock Primal Hurl Art Therapy Group for Particularly Messy Serial Killers.

Luckily, my friends are more broadminded than me. I parade their best stuff in public and they don't get all twisted about it. The Polish poet Czeslaw Milosz once said that when a writer is born into a family, the family is finished. Equally, when a columnist has bosom friends, they find that they no longer have a thing to call their own.

Every anecdote they utter goes directly into the writer's mental dressing-up box, and though any single item may not re-emerge for a decade, it will undoubtedly turn up again one day – albeit crumpled, stained, mildewed, or laced with holes

– to the owner's muffled astonished cry of 'But surely that was *mine* originally, wasn't it?'

It is no extenuation whatever to claim (as I do, frequently) that so long as I attribute stories to 'a friend'; so long as I don't tell the story *against* the originator – well, then it's all perfectly OK. In her Great Left-Behind Coat Ethics Research, my friend encountered precisely such casuistical chicanery, and I poured scorn on all of it.

For instance, perhaps it would be a different ethical kettle of fish if the item were not a coat but a frock? Or if the owner were the sort of person who suffers from amnesia? Or if you only allowed yourself to wear the coat outdoors on National No Decorating Day? Bah, I retorted; the matter is simple. If it doesn't belong to you, leave it in a cupboard. The rest is sophistry.

And so here I am, writing about my friend's article about borrowing things without asking. And did I ask her? Of course I didn't.

'Yes! This will do nicely!' I yelled excitedly, as I tried it on for size, did a quick twirl, and hacked a few inches off the sleeves with the bread-knife. Such a gigantic fuss about nothing! As the great Nobel Prize winner Czeslaw Milosz might have remarked, if they didn't want me to wear it, they really shouldn't have left it lying about.

⸎

At the cinema these days there is a rather peculiar advert for jeans. It is basically a witty rewriting of *Cinderella*, but since it appears to have been edited by a madman run wild with a bacon- slicer, the narrative unfolds so precipitately that it takes at least two viewings to get the gist. Anyway, it goes something like this. Clock strikes bong for midnight. Boy rushes off without his jeans. Girl holds jeans to face with funny wistful-but-determined look in her eyes, then hawks jeans around town, getting big fat men to try them on. Finally, she locates her beloved, who buttons up a treat. And that's it. Allowing for how difficult it is to make trousers even slightly interesting, this ad is a huge success.

The thing about fairy tales, surely, is that they can be used to sell anything; indeed, it is almost their primary function. Anyone who thinks it is radical of the Disney studio to turn the heroine of *Beauty and the Beast* into a modern-thinking self-determined book-lover ('There must be more than this provincial life!' she sings discontentedly, several times) is right in only one respect. Yes, it is radical *of the Disney studio*. Previously Disney sold other things; now it is selling this. A generation of girls grew up believing that to be a heroine (Cinderella, Snow White, Sleeping Beauty) all you required were a decent whistling technique, first-class handiness with a broom, and an ability to sleep for extended periods in a glass box without mussing your make-up or dribbling on your frock. And as values go, these were probably OK for the time.

But my point is this. In the traditional folk tale, women were not these puny types. Big tears did not roll down their pretty faces, and they did not wear rouge. Instead, they rescued princes from enchantment, tipped witches into ovens, all that. The reason we know only of the rescue-me namby-pambies is that we inherit our knowledge of folk tales from the Victorians, whose respect for divergent viewpoints, especially in the realm of sexual politics, was notoriously meagre. Funny how *The Sleeping Prince* got dropped from the canon, wasn't it? I wonder why.

But as Alison Lurie points out in her marvellous book on children's literature, *Don't Tell the Grown-Ups*, even the Grimm brothers tidied up the tales to reflect the mores. 'In each subsequent edition of the tales,' writes Lurie, 'women were given less to say and do.' At issue, of course, is whether it is cynical and outrageous to impose modern values on traditional stories. When George Cruikshank, the Victorian illustrator, rewrote four of his favourite fairy stories as temperance tracts, Charles Dickens countered with a brilliant essay, 'Frauds on the Fairies' (1853), denouncing the practice. But what is odd now is to see how certain Dickens was that the versions he remembered from childhood were necessarily the originals. Cruikshank, thundered Dickens, 'has altered the text of a fairy story; and against his right to do any such thing we protest with all our might and main ... Whosoever alters them to suit his own opinions, whatever they are, is guilty of an act of presumption, and appropriates to himself what does not belong to him.'

Dickens boiled with sarcasm ('Imagine a Total Abstinence edition of *Robinson Crusoe*, with the rum left out. Imagine a Peace edition, with the gunpowder left out, and the rum left in'); and then embarked on a thoroughly sardonic rewrite of *Cinderella* incorporating absurdly modish references to tax reform, vegetarianism and, interestingly, the rights of women. Cinderella, in this version, was a moral swot and reviler of meat, who on becoming queen did all sorts of absurdly fashionable things. She 'threw open the right of voting, and of being elected to public offices, and of making the laws, to the whole of her sex; who thus came to be always gloriously occupied with public life and *whom nobody dared to love*'. It is the mark of a great writer that he allows his own imagination to scare him like this. Come to think of it, this must have been the version that was read to the infant Neil Lyndon in his cot.

Where does it all stop? Well, it won't stop at all, of course. Walt Disney is supposed to have said, 'People don't want fairy stories the way they were written. In the end they'll probably remember the story the way we film it anyway.' But now Linda Woolverton, the scriptwriter of Disney's *Beauty and the Beast*, has started saying she would like to remake 'the old Disneys', so it turns out that nothing is sacred after all. Cinderella, she says, needs to stand up to the ugly sisters, stop hanging around with mice, and not necessarily marry the prince. Hmm. Snow White should not stay at home all day but work with her chums in the mines and marry one of the vertically challenged men with pickaxes. And lastly, Sleeping Beauty – the most famously inert character of them all – should 'track down and person- ally punish' her wicked stepmother immediately she wakes up in the glass box. Whether she will punish her stepmother by making her watch the new version of Cinderella is not made clear.

I promise I didn't make any of this up. I just wonder how serious Linda Woolverton was when she said it. Currently she has been let loose by Disney on a remake of the famous animal adventure film The Incredible Journey, which seems at first glance to have fewer opportunities for political correctness, although the cat could have a wooden leg. Meanwhile, it ought to be said that Belle may indeed be a book-reader, who swoons at the sight of the Beast's enormous library, yet she is a traditional heroine in most other respects. She is kind, friendly, chats with cockney teapots, and has enormous eyes. And of course she is everso, everso pretty. But then 'Passable Looking and the Beast' doesn't have quite the same ring to it somehow.

⌒

Anyone watching the BBC news on Sunday night, with its edited highlights of the Remembrance Day ceremony, will have noted a very curious thing. The newsmen cut out the two minutes' silence. Thus, the clock went 'Bong', the distant cannon went 'Bang', and the next thing you knew, they were playing the Last Post and laying wreaths. Since the annual two minutes' reflective silence is about the most moving thing on television, it is possible that the edit was intended to protect the already raw feelings of the grief-stricken. But I doubt it. What we witnessed here was the consequence of fear, of a feeble failure of nerve. You see, silence on the television is about as unthinkable (Oh no!) as blank lines in a newspaper, thus:

In fact, the chances of this gaping white wound not being panic-sutured by someone in the course of the paper's production ('What the hell is this? There's a *space* on page 18!') are very slim indeed, and I am thoroughly foolhardy even to attempt it.

Gaps are great, however. I firmly believe we should have more gaps, especially in broadcasting. 'And now on BBC2, er, *Nothing*. Over on BBC1, in just over ten minutes, good grief, *Nothing* there, as well.' Personally, I would embrace the return of the potter's wheel, the interval bell, the test card, and the inventive use of 'Normal Programmes Will be Resumed Shortly', but arguably *Nothing* could be finer. Don't other people's brains get overloaded? Or is it only mine? Has no one else noticed that new books are published every week, without let-up, over and over, till the end of creation? Why don't they stop sometimes? Why don't they admit they have run out of ideas? Am I run mad, or just in desperate need of a holiday? Asked recently in a published questionnaire to compose a headline for the event that I would most like to cover, I'm afraid I gave myself away completely. 'Airwaves eerily silent,' I wrote, 'as all networks simultaneously run out of programmes.'

Clearly this is an unusual attitude to our splendiferous burgeoning culture, especially in a television critic, but on the other hand, for God's sake somebody, *help*! While others famously 'surf' through the television channels – presumably humming 'Catch a Wave' by the Beach Boys as they paddle back out, letting their fingertips stiffen from prolonged immersion – I find I can only cope by taking short exhilarating dips, then towelling off vigorously and getting fully dressed again. Sharing a sofa (and a remote control) with someone who uses commercial breaks in cop shows as an opportunity to surf over and 'see what's happening in the snooker' is guaranteed, in fact, to drive me to violence.

'Shouldn't we switch back now?' I say, after a minute has passed.

'Not yet, this is interesting.' Pause.

'Let's switch back, go on.'

'Not yet.' A longer pause, more charged with tension. There is an irritating click of balls.

'Give me that thing!' I shout, suddenly. 'I want to go back to *Columbo*!'

At which point a grabbing-and-kicking scuffle breaks out, and the remote control is somehow hurled out of the window, where it lands with a plop in a rain-butt.

Recently on Radio 4 the wonderfully repugnant Alan Partridge (spoof Pringle-wearing radio personality chat-show host) attempted a one-minute silence, when an interviewee supposedly suffered a fatal heart attack in the chair opposite. 'And now, the one minute's silence,' said Partridge (or something similar). 'Yes, ah-ha, here we go ... very respectful, this ... in case you're wondering, anyone who's just tuned in ... this is a One Minute Silence ... about half-way through, I should think ... it's very moving, actually ... perhaps I could use this opportunity to tell you about next week's show ... or perhaps not ... can't be long now ... that's it! Minute's up! Lovely.' Well, I'd just like to say I genuinely appreciated what he was trying to do. So here's another gap:

I hope you enjoyed it as much as I did.

⁀

Once, when I was still a literary editor, I was instructed by an ebullient boss to commission a piece from Norman Mailer. 'Try

Norman Mailer,' he said. 'If our usual fee isn't high enough, tell him we can add an extra fifty quid.' I dropped the tray of cups I was holding. 'Something wrong?' he said. Fighting back tears, I forced out the words, 'Isseny nnuff.' 'What's that?' he said. 'Isseny NNUFF.' 'Oh, you never know,' said my cheery editor, patting me on the shoulder. 'Tell you what: you can add a hundred. That ought to do it.' And he went off home.

The trouble with having low self-esteem is that you recognize immediately when you are out of your depth. I was out of mine from the moment the Manhattan switchboard-operator took my call. 'You're calling from *where*?' she asked, making me repeat myself more loudly, so that she could hold up the receiver for everyone else to have a good laugh, too. As I felt myself sinking, I realized I was like a character in an American short story, hazarding everything on the tiny chance that someone had once saved Mailer's life by staunching a gunshot wound with a copy of The Listener.

Mailer's agent was clearly a very busy man, with little time to mess around with small fry like me. When he at last spoke to me, I was convinced he was having a haircut and manicure at the same time. He started with the bottom line: 'You ought to know,' he declared equably, 'that Norman's alimony commitments are so titanic that if he writes for anything below his bottom rate he actually ends up in court for defaulting. Now, I'll tell you that the last time Norman wrote for a magazine, he was paid fifty thousand dollars. Tell me what you are offering and I'll run it past him.'

I did a rapid calculation on a scrap-pad, and figured we were roughly forty-nine and a half thousand dollars short. Did I have sufficient *cojones* to pledge the magazine into bankruptcy? No I did not. I added an extra hundred to our top fee ('I can always sell the car,' I thought), but my effort elicited no cheers or huzzahs from the agent. As he said goodbye, I heard myself say, 'Don't you want to know what we'd like him to write about?' but it was too late. I hung up and went home. I never found out whether he ran it past Norman or not, but I have often envisaged it bowling past Mailer at top speed, just as he was bending down to tie his shoelaces.

I have dwelt on this conversation ever since. None of it need be true, of course: the agent may just have been trying to let me down gently. But what a terrible fix for poor Norman. It struck me that we might turn the evidence to our advantage, by printing a slogan across the mast-head: 'The magazine Norman Mailer can't afford to write for'. But though I ran this idea past the editor, he didn't attempt to flag it down.

Contrary to popular preconception, you can meet all sorts on a march to save Radio 4 Long Wave. Oh yes. On Saturday, as our happy band of orderly middle-class protesters set off from Speakers' Corner and headed for Broadcasting House, I actually found myself demonstrating alongside a woman who reads the *Guardian*. Hey! Right! So let us, once and for all, forget this slur that the Long Wave Campaign is about fuddy-duddy types who think 'grass roots' is something to do with *Gardeners' Question Time*. What Saturday's protest showed was that it is possible to feel very strongly about an issue yet remain polite, that's all. 'What do we want?' yelled our cheerleader. 'Radio 4!' we responded, slightly heady at our own daring. 'Where do we want it?' 'Long Wave!' 'How do we ask?' 'Please!'

It was a small march, admittedly, but the hell with it, we carried lots of balloons. Efforts to recruit bystanders from Oxford Street ('Come and join us!') were slightly optimistic, I thought – the bewildered looks of shoppers telling us what we knew in our hearts already: that the cause of 'R4 LW' is not an instantly emotive one, and that the joke about Duke

Hussey being able to pick up FM reception on his leg is a trifle arcane.

'What are you protesting about?' a young woman asked the contingent from Belgium. 'The BBC wants to put Radio 4 on FM only, which means we won't get it on the Continent any more.' The woman walked alongside us while she considered this information, in all its many aspects. 'That's terrible,' she said at last, as she nevertheless noticeably slowed her pace and dropped out. 'Hey, listen, I hope you get what you want.' And then, as an afterthought, she called after us, 'This Radio 4, can you get it here?'

There were contingents from all over the place – all of northern Europe, and lots of areas in Britain where trying to get an FM signal is almost as fruitless and frustrating as trying to get a straight answer from the BBC. Embarrassed that personally I did not live in a far-flung outpost of the Long Wave Diaspora, I admitted *sotto voce* to my exotic *Guardian*-reading friend that my FM reception is actually OK so long as I don't attempt to move the radio, or stand more than three feet away from it in leather-soled shoes. She seemed relieved. She admitted likewise that hers was also OK, so long as everyone in the kitchen made only limited lateral movements with their upper bodies, and the fridge door was left open.

Neither of us, however, could get FM in our bathrooms, so we formed an instant bond and became the Bathroom Contingent, marching on behalf of Long Wave bathrooms throughout the land. Meanwhile I couldn't help inwardly pondering the health consequences of repeatedly opening the fridge for the sake of good bits on *Pick of the Week*. John Birt's BBC no doubt has many things on its conscience, but the potential for dealing bacteriological food-poisoning to a nation of *Guardian* readers has surely escaped its purview until now.

When we arrived at Broadcasting House, our reception – appropriately enough – was a bit fuzzy, and depended on where you were standing. Suddenly mob-like once we stopped moving, we assembled outside the Langham Hotel and raised our educated voices against those unresponsive grey stone walls, waggling our balloons in an aggressive manner, until eventually a bloke in a suit (Phil Harding) came out to meet us and shoved through the crowd, filmed by BBC news. And that was it; the balloons were collected; we all drifted off to John Lewis for a bit of light shopping. According to reports in the Sunday papers, Mr Harding said, 'I'm listening; I'm listening,' but I didn't hear him. Perhaps I was wearing the wrong shoes.

But what I will remember is the weird experience of waiting across the road for something to happen. Extra police materialized – making us feel more agitated, of course – and we started to grow restive. After all, if there was one thing guaranteed to make us livid, it was the feeling of being ignored by the BBC. I had a nasty moment, I can tell you, when it suddenly struck me that if a riot broke out I might go down in broadcasting history as a member of the Bathroom Two.

Since supermarket shopping is probably the most dismal, routine, mindless, time-wasting and wrist-slitting element in most people's lives, it was at first glance rather baffling to discover that ITV was planning Supermarket Sweep, a weekday morning game show in which contestants are tested (and rewarded) on their ability to answer simple questions about products and then hurtle down the aisles, lobbing big cartons of washing-powder into overloaded trolleys amid whoops of excitement from a studio audience. 'Oh heavenly doo-dahs, that the culture should be reduced to this,' I sighed (in a vague, regretful kind of way): 'Stop the world, I want to get off; to have seen what I have seen, see what I see.' Admittedly shopping is a skill (some people are certainly better at it than others), but as an intellectual test, you have to admit, it's just one small step from asking people to spell their own name, or open their own front door and switch the light on.

QUESTION: It's eaten from a plastic bowl on the floor, by a pet that likes to go for walks.
ANSWER (*tentatively*): Dog? Er, dog? Is it?
Q: Hmm, I'll let you have it, but the answer I really wanted was dog *food*.
A: Ah. Yes. I see.

The first *Supermarket Sweep* was shown yesterday, and yes, the above exchange did take place, no kidding. Of course, the programme's proceedings bore no relation to supermarket shopping in the real nightmare, universal sense (which would have made it interesting): none of the trolleys were fixed so that they slewed violently sideways into the biscuits; no mad people blocked the aisles muttering over a basket of teabags and kitchen roll. The real skill in supermarket shopping is to get round (and out) without the banality of the experience reducing you to screams or blackouts. But none of this was reflected in *Supermarket Sweep*, which was the opposite of shopping anyway, because the strategy was to locate only the most expensive stuff, and eschew the bargains. How interesting, moreover, that the climactic 'checkout' section was cunningly edited for highlights, so we never found out whether the contestants were obliged to yawn and stare at the ceiling while a clueless overalled youth disappeared with their unmarked tin of beans, and then, once out of view, decided to forsake this humdrum life and catch a plane to Guatemala.

Politically, I get confused by programmes such as this. If the idea is to make uneducated people feel good about themselves, it churns up highly equivocal feelings of, on the one hand, 'Right on, give them a chance!' and on the other, 'Could we please go back to the eighteenth-century notion of improvement and start again?' In the modern world, careless congratulatory talk has been taken literally, with appalling results. 'You ought to be on the stage' was a thoughtless cliché that led straight to karaoke; 'You ought to be on the telly' led to Jeremy Beadle; and ultimately, 'You're so good at shopping, you ought to go on *Mastermind*' led, in the very last tick-tock minutes of civilization, as the hourglass sands drained finally and softly away, to *Supermarket Sweep*. Personally, I reckon I know the ground-floor layout of John Lewis so intimately I could traverse it blindfold. But it's odd to think there's any intrinsic virtue in that. Rather the reverse, really: it's the shameful sign of a misspent adulthood.

The additionally consoling thing for the *Supermarket Sweep* contestants, of course, is that they can beat the brainboxes in their own arena. Just think, if you put Eric Korn and Irene Thomas (the legendary *Round Britain Quiz* London team) in this grab-a-trolley-and-run situation, they would almost certainly be rubbish. Told to collect 'Tuna and sweetcorn cottage cheese, a litre of bleach, and high-juice lemon squash,' they would pause and frown, musing, putting two and two together, while the others bolted for the shelves in tracksuit and trainers, and performed heroic wheelies by the fridge. 'Sweetcorn. Mm. Bleach. Lemons,' says Irene Thomas with a happy quizzical overtone, indicating that she's spotted the arcane link between these disparate items already. 'Would *Der Rosenkavalier* help us here? Yes, I thought it would ...' Oh dear. And the answer he wanted was dog food. It just goes to show the limits of a classical education.

In times of stress, I firmly believe, you must reach for the family Bible, close your eyes tight, allow the book to drop open, and stab the page forcefully with a compass point wielded in a random arc. The idea is not just that the violence of the act will make you feel better (although it does), but that fortune will somehow guide you to a relevant helpful passage, while at the same time miraculously preventing you from impaling your other hand to the desk.

Superstitious? Certainly, and especially the last bit. But I am sure I have seen evidence of its efficacy, if only in the movies. You know: gangsters staring agape in shock when the book falls open at 'Be sure your sin will find you out' (Numbers xxxii, 23) just seconds before a curtained window is suddenly blown to smithereens a couple of feet behind them.

Anyway, spending a lot of time on my own, I sometimes devote the odd couple of hours to testing the theory of Bible-dropping, rather as if I were an infinite number of monkeys bent on disproving the notion of dramatic genius. The happy sound of 'Wump! Slash! Ah-hah!' sometimes emanates from my flat all day long. Where other people might, as a matter of course, consult Patric Walker or the I Ching (or Spillikins) before applying for a job or taking a trip abroad, there are days when I scarcely plan a journey to the post box without first securing some random canonical go-ahead from Deuter-onomy in the Authorized Version.

I don't take it seriously, not really. But on the other hand I have had some pretty startling results. Take the other day. I had been experimenting in the kitchen again, had concocted a rather interesting Lentil and Pink Marshmallow Bolognese in a saucepan. Obviously I now required guidance: should I take a picture of it before slinging it in the bin? I shut my eyes, flipped open the Good Book, poked it with the bread knife, and what do you think it said? It said: 'What is this that thou hast done?' (Genesis iii, 13). Blimey. How spooky. I tried it again. 'Wump! Slash! Ah-hah!' And this time I got II Kings iv, 40: 'There is death in the pot.'

Sometimes the messages are a bit mysterious. Once, when I had been drawing losers for hours – 'Go up, thou bald head' (?); 'And they spoiled the Egyptians' (?) – and wumping and slashing like an early agricultural machine in *Tess of the D'Urbervilles*, I suddenly got a rather grumpy-sounding 'As a dog returneth to his vomit, so a fool returneth to his folly' (Proverbs xxvi, 11), which drew me up short for a minute. Some significance here, perhaps? Naturally, I decided to have another go. And this time I got 'The dog is turned to his vomit *again*' (II Peter ii, 22). Weird, eh? But completely unfathomable, alas.

Anyway, the reason I mention all this is that I recently discovered a potential application for this unusual hobby of mine. Browsing in a religious bookshop one rainy afternoon, and flicking through Bibles ('Why stand ye here all the day idle?' met my gaze immediately, so I knew things were running to form), I discovered a rack of biblical posters. And much as I dislike slander in matters of taste, these posters were truly horrid – in the classical sense of making all your hair stick out like spines on a hedgehog. Who could be responsible for these ghastly things, I wondered. I could only suppose that the infinite number of monkeys had been up to their usual tricks.

Imagine, if you will, two large fluffy ducklings waddling away down a country lane at sunset, with underneath the legend 'Can two walk together, except they be agreed?' I mean, is this sick, or what? A pair of cute kids hold hands in a lush pasture, bathed in summer light, and one holds out a daisy-chain to the other. 'God loveth a cheerful giver,' it says. Two tiger cubs embrace roughly, evidently mindful of the injunction of 'Let not the sun go down upon your wrath.' I ask you, what a paltry use of the imagination. I nearly produced some new vomit to come back to later on.

But on the other hand, I did rush home with a whole new sense of purpose. My idea was simple: take this ghastly notion to its natural bathetic extreme. A man could be shown reprimanding a cat that has unaccountably stalked out of the room halfway through the *EastEnders* omnibus: 'What,' he says, in a speech bubble, 'could ye not watch with me one hour?' Good, eh? A woman, evidently frazzled from shopping, could be shown consulting a list in a dusty foreign market, and looking jolly peeved. 'Is there no balm in Gilead?' could be written underneath.

I hope my posters will give pleasure somewhere. Meanwhile I shall cheerfully continue with my Bible-bashing. I got 'We have as it were brought forth wind' the other day (Isaiah xxvi, 18), and I can't say it hasn't given me lots to think about. An acquaintance has gently suggested to me that any big book – telephone directory, Argos Catalogue – will work equally well for my purposes, but I suspect this is a fallacy. Faced with a dilemma, surely nobody wants to know that the answer is an automatic pet-feeder at £12.99, or 'Mr H. MacGuire, 26 Fulwell Gardens, W6'. Unless of course (by some remote probability) you are Mrs MacGuire, suffering from amnesia. Or you have suddenly acquired an infinite number of monkeys, all demanding meals at funny intervals.

It is only when one watches several weeks of 'Crime and Punishment' television that one realizes how little real-life contact one has with the police. It is rather odd. As a viewer, I feel I am so well acquainted with police procedure I could confidently head a murder enquiry; but at the same time, in real life, I have only twice been inside a police station. Talking recently to the producer of a 'Cops on the Box' documentary, I was relieved to find he shared this wildly discrepant experience. In making his programme, he said, he hired two actors in uniform to sit in an old white Zephyr (in homage to Z Cars) and walk shoulder-to-shoulder down whitewashed corridors. At one point, he momentarily forgot where he was, turned round to see these two coppers bearing down on him, and jumped aloft with shock.

Perhaps this explains why it has stuck in my mind, the time long ago when a real-life local CID bloke, taking a statement from me about a bag-snatching, conformed to his image as portrayed by left-wing television playwrights and thereby delivered a bit of a jolt. He had asked what my job was, to which I truthfully replied I was a literary editor on a magazine (The Listener). He looked interested, so I elaborated. Publishers sent me their new books, I said, and I commissioned reviews; then I edited them, wrote headlines, laid out pages and corrected proofs. 'It's a dog's life,' I added cheerfully, in case he thought I was showing off. He thought about it, as if he were going to volunteer for a spot of reviewing (people often did), and then pronounced the words that have niggled me ever since: 'I expect there's room for corruption in that.' I remember how my mind went blank. I said how d'you mean, corruption? You've got something people want, he said; it stands to reason they'll pay for it.

Well naturally I went back to the office next day and shook all the books to see if any fivers fell out, but with no success. I rang up Chatto & Windus and asked for the bribe department, but they denied all knowledge. My detective was evidently wrong in his suspicions. But what alarmed me, obviously, was that this friendly backhander insinuation was the first conversational angle he thought of. While normal people might have said, 'Do you read all the books?', 'What's Stephen Fry like?' or 'So that's why you smell of book dust and Xerox toner!', this policeman evidently saw the world as one huge greasy palm, and assumed that everyone else did, too. In retrospect I wish I had countered more effectively. 'Detective sergeant, are you?' I might have said, 'Gosh, I expect there's room for reading a novel with a pencil in your hand in that.'

So it took me aback, this encounter, the way corruption came up in the first five minutes I ever spent with a policeman. Especially when, merely out of politeness, I turned the conversation round to him ('But I expect there's room for corruption in *your* job?') and he fobbed me off with a ludicrous story involving a motorist and a ten-bob note. 'You seem to have left this money in your driving-licence, sir; we must be more careful,' he had said, apparently, handing it back confused.

In my more paranoid moments I still wonder, though, whether I missed out on something. Whether other literary editors were taking delivery of string bags stuffed with notes in the gents at Waterloo while I was miserably sticking galleys on to layout sheets and getting cow-gum in my eyebrows. The idea of the lit. ed. as wide-boy certainly has its attractions; any gathering of the downtrodden, stoop-gaited chaps (it's mostly chaps) tells you at a glance that sniffing the bindings is the nearest they get to an illicit activity. So what we obviously require is a culture in which literary editing, not police work, is the theme of tough, uncompromising television shows. 'I told you,' the hard-boiled lit. ed. snarls down the phone, while admiring his manicured nails, 'I want a pony for the Brookner, or the deal's off.' The viewing nation would be held in thrall. He's tough; he's mean; he edits book reviews. And then, whenever the public chanced to meet a real literary editor in the flesh, they would get the same frisson of second-hand recognition that we currently reserve for the cops.

☞

At the end of last year, when the terrific Radio 4 dramatization of *Little Women* was underway on Thursday mornings (tough luck for people with jobs), a man wrote to *Woman's Hour* with an interesting point. Listeners had been challenged to vote on which of Louisa May Alcott's four March sisters, Meg, Jo, Beth, Amy, they identified with – which possibly doesn't sound very interesting, but actually was. For example, some women curiously opted for Meg (sweet, placid, forgettable), and a few even fancied themselves as the vain affected Amy or the timid moribund Beth. However, the majority opted for the splendid heroine Jo – tomboy, literary genius, portrait of the author as a stormy petrel – perhaps because she seems quite modern, but more likely because identification with Jo is what the author so clearly intends. Like a fool, I hadn't realized this before. I thought I was the only reader who secretly admired Jo March. But it turns out that the adult female world is crammed with undercover Jo fans, all wishing we could scribble up a storm, scorch our frocks, and exclaim 'Christopher Columbus!' despite its not being ladylike.

If these names and characters mean nothing to you, I can only say you must blame your classical education. These are female archetypes, mate. How can you possibly understand feminism if you don't personally recollect the quietly touching scene in which good, wise Mrs March (known as 'Marmee') advises her justly furious daughter 'Never let the sun go down on your anger'? Generations of young female readers have felt so exasperated at this point that they immediately chained themselves to railings or resolved to set fire to something. It all goes very deep. 'Moral pap for the young' was how Louisa May Alcott once startlingly described her own books, and the suggestion of a soft, absorbent foodstuff shovelled into girl infants is alarmingly close to the truth as one recalls it. Radio 4's decision to present *Little Women* and then its sequel *Good Wives* (which finished last week, amid sobs in my house, with Jo's marriage to the penniless Professor Bhaer) was a brilliant one, if only as a kind of catharsis therapy. All those forgotten, repressed episodes somehow fundamental to one's own childhood were dug up publicly and found not to be so ghastly after all.

But what did this chap write in his letter to *Woman's Hour*, you want to know. Well, he said that having read *Little Women* at an early age, not only had he found it useful in understanding women, but he had honestly needed to enquire no further. As far as female taxonomy went, Meg, Jo, Beth and Amy covered the lot. If an occasional hybrid crossed his path (a Meg-Beth, an Amy-Jo-Marmee), it was the work of an instant to sort it into its constituent parts. He spoke as someone who had known multitudes of women – but each of them for a shortish period, presumably, the acquaintance always mysteriously ceasing at the precise moment when she discovered his heavily anno-tated copy of *Little Women* wedged behind the lavatory-cistern, sussed his creepy game at once and scarpered via the back gate into the sunshine. No woman should stick around with a man who thinks she's Beth, it's obvious. When I was twelve years old and chronically ill, my older sister cheerfully said that she saw me as a little Beth, and in my innocence I thought she was being nice. But I realize now the sad, sad truth of the matter, that actually she wanted me to croak.

Four seems to be the standard number for female types: four sisters in *What Katy Did*; four Marys in the famous *Bunty* comic strip; four Golden Girls. When a pilot for a British version of *The Golden Girls* was broadcast recently, the makers obviously couldn't think of any new female comic humours to depict, so they adhered to the American originals – vain, dim, sardonic, outrageous – so endorsing the unfortunate impression that this is the full range available. Perhaps the number four gives the illusion of all-round choice; I mean, it always worked for Opal Fruits. For the moment, however, I am far too worried about this long-buried identification with Jo March to give it much thought. Good grief, it may even explain why I am disastrously attracted to old foreign blokes with no money.

⌒

If I were Barbie, I would be rather hurt by the general reception given to my new dance work-out video. Amid all the hoots of derision, nobody bothers to see its significance from Barbie's own point of view – her amazing courage, after those years in a creative desert, to 'pick up the pieces' and 'go out on a limb'. It's not easy being Barbie, you know. For one thing, how would *you* like it if your boy-friend (Ken) slept in a shoe-box, and melted on contact with radiators? You would feel pretty humiliated, obviously. But remember the publishing disaster of *Fear of Bending*, Barbie's teensy-weensy, reveal-all autobiography? Remember her public miniature fury when Claire Bloom snatched the lead in *A Doll's House*? Those drunken pavement cat-fights with Tressy outside a small-scale model of the Limelight Club? Those whispers about the itsy-bitsy Betty Ford Clinic? Ah yes, it all comes back to you now, when it's too late, the damage done.

So why shouldn't she issue a dance work-out video? One thing to be said for Barbie is that she always kept her figure. Obviously there is a slight danger that if you adhered to Barbie's rigorous hamstring exercises you might end up with your feet (like hers) permanently pointed in a tip-toe – which means that unless you wear the right high heels, you forever topple forwards and bang your bonce. But otherwise Barbie possesses precisely the same qualities as the other supermodels, whose exercise videos are bestsellers. She is plastic, perfect, self-absorbed, and her hair comes ready-lacquered. However, she is also very, very small; so you can derive a certain comfort from the thought that Richard Gere wouldn't glance at her twice (unless he crunched her underfoot by mistake).

Whether I shall buy *Dance Work-Out With Barbie* depends on my next fortnightly visit to the 'Body Sculpt' class, led by 'Geri' at the local gym. A young woman whose abductor muscles are strung so tightly that they are visibly teetering on the edge of a breakdown, Geri is beginning to annoy me. She is Australian, white-blonde, long-legged and deep-tanned, with a face like Rosanna Arquette. She wears skimpy Lycra ensembles in purple and lime green with large interesting peep-holes cut from the sides, just to show that in places where the rest of us have grey-white crêpey stuff (which cries aloud for elasticated containment, 'Pants! Give us pants!'), she has taut brown skin, and that's all. I am beginning to hate the body sculpt class. Sometimes I catch a glimpse of myself in the wall-to-wall mirror, lumbering out of step, and I think, 'I don't have to do this, *Woodrow Wyatt doesn't do this.*' Which shows to what levels of mental desiccation an envy of somebody's lime-green peep-holes can plunge you.

Barbie's work-out is for five-year-olds, of course. But so, in a way, is the body sculpt class. In fact, few experiences in adult life so readily evoke the wretched emotions of the infants' playground as to be led in a mindless game of mimicry by a tyrannical bimbo shouting above the music, 'Do this! Now do that! Back to this, again! Four of these! Two and two! Left leg, right leg, right leg, left leg! Left leg, right leg, right leg, left leg!' Noticeably, there is no camaraderie among Geri's brutalized troupe – just as there is none when you are five years old – so you can't heckle 'Make your mind up, woman!' and expect to get a laugh and a breather. Under Geri's tutelage, the goody-goodies get all the steps right, the others do their earnest best, while I, the only no-hoper, clap my hands at the wrong moments and pray privately that the bell will soon ring for Two-Times Tables or Finger-Painting.

I wish Barbie success with her video. Children don't need it, obviously, but it will be good for the rest of us to face facts.

See this dolly? This is what you want to look like. This is what Geri looks like. But in any other context she'd look very, very stupid. Apparently, in the video, Barbie doesn't do much of the actual dancing; someone called Kim takes over. Meanwhile Barbie presumably has a lie-down, phones her analyst, and then smokes a minuscule cigarette from a tiny box. Honestly, if this is a role-model for today's children, I think we have little to fear.

It is a well-established fact (not acknowledged enough) that in journalism there are only eleven basic ideas. The reason journalists over the age of twenty-five get cynical and start to fall over in public houses is that in their cradles they have been cursed with a particular kind of limited intelligence. They are bright people, but a Bad Fairy has ensured that they are bright enough only to discover the eleven basic ideas for themselves. What they are not bright enough to notice is that everything they do has been done before. Then one day they realize – to the dismay of the Really Good Fairy who gave them the brains – that they have run out of ideas. Disillusioned, they are obliged to stand back and watch as other, younger people – the fairy-dust still sparkling on their shoulders – start to discover the eleven ideas all over again.

New ideas are, therefore, pretty exciting things within journalism, and I can't remember the last time anybody had one. But as an example of how desperate everybody is, let us take the example of the word 'Bratpack'. Within minutes of its coining, this term had been picked up and applied to just about everybody – movie directors, teenage actors, Manhattan writers – before finally coming to rest in the *Loose Ends* studio in Broadcasting House. That was just the beginning. The next day somebody said, 'Yeah, but how about "Ratpack" as a term for the media journalists who write about (and occasionally join) the "Bratpack"?' Brilliant, as Basil Fawlty might say, Brilliant. The richness of imagination was of such quality that even the originators themselves seemed impressed.

So I thought I'd join in, get a share of the action, start an entirely original (if a bit derivative) genus of nomenclature. We all want to make our mark, and this seems a simple enough method of doing it.

My first thought was that one could refer to all clever French writers – de Beauvoir, Sartre, Camus – as the 'Baccalauréat-pack'. What do you think? By the same token Indians, like Jhabvala, Narayan and Desai, might be called the 'Ghatpack' (not to be confused with the American tough-guy detective grouping 'Gatpack'). On a more serious note, writers publishing their work secretly in totalitarian states might be called, simply, the 'Samizdatpack'. Smartipants writers might be termed the 'Eclatpack', while successful, well-heeled NW3-based novel-a-year writers could rejoice in any of the following: 'Cravatpack', 'VATpack', or, well, 'Fatpack'. This only leaves the blockbuster writers, who, I think, can be pretty neatly summed up in the term 'Tatpack'.

So there you are. A complete new terminology. Please watch out for any appearance of these terms, for which copyright application is already in the post.

☙

On Sunday morning, a thirty-eight-year-old unpublished poet named Clive was mournfully twiddling a pencil at his special poetry-composing desk, huddled in a greatcoat, when the telephone rang. He paused before answering it, feeling sorry for himself. 'Nothing rhymes with telephone,' he said, his face puckering uncontrollably; 'in fact, why do I bother?' He picked up the receiver. 'Hello?' he croaked.

It was his mother. She sounded agitated. Clive, alarmed, snapped his pencil in half, and then looked at it, aghast.

'Clive, I'm worried,' she said. 'Have you read today's *Sunday Times*?'

'Of course not.'

'Then you don't know! Oh, that I should have to break such news to my own son! Clive, it says here that a professor in America – is Kentucky still in America? I expect so – has established from studying a thousand important twentieth-century dead people that poets are by far the most at-risk group for depression, paranoia and suicide!'

'Yes?' Clive shrugged. 'So what?'

'So you never told me that! You said, "Mum, I want to be a poet," and I let you! You were so sweet, with those big brown eyes, Clive, and you said, "If I can't be a poet, Mum, I'll kill myself." And now I discover you've chosen the very profession in which the risk is greatest! You tricked me, Clive!'

'You're hysterical.'

'Who is this Sylvia Plath he mentions? Is she a friend of yours? What about W.H. Auden? Is he making you depressed, too? Give up this poetry madness, my son, before it is too late!'

Clive spent the rest of the day indoors. Like Jean Cocteau, he knew that poetry was indispensable, although indispensable to what exactly, he didn't feel qualified to say. He was deeply offended by the sweeping accusation of poet-paranoia, yet didn't dare go out to buy the newspaper, for fear he would find an immense placard outside the shop, screaming 'Poets Are Loonies! Official!' So instead he wearily copied out some of his old verses – in his best wiggly handwriting, on lined paper – and made packages to send to *Marxism Today* and *The Economist*, choosing 'Lines on the Wedding of Prince Andrew to Lady Sarah Ferguson (revised)' and 'Why Is This Black Dog Following Me Around? – An Allegory'. He didn't know whether these magazines printed poetry, though he somehow felt sure they used to. Last week his submissions to *The Listener* and *Punch* had both been returned with just the bald, scribbled legend, 'Not known at this address'. Clive had taken these harsh rebuffs very much to heart.

Suddenly, at about six o'clock, the phone rang again. It was his mother. 'Clive. I've been looking at this article, and you've got to tell me something. Were you gloomy by the time you were thirteen?'

'Gloomy?'

'Just answer the question.'

'Well, yes. I suppose I've always been ...'

'So it's not the job that makes you depressed? It's because you're sensitive, or high-minded or something, that you chose this particular job in the first place?'

'But poetry isn't a job, Mum, more a result of a struggle in the poet's mind between something he wants to express and the medium in which he intends to express it.'

There was a pause.

'Why do you always talk like that, Clive? Do you think Albert Einstein talked to his mother like that? No, he didn't. And why? Because he wasn't a wimp of a poet, depressed all the time!' She hung up.

Clive wondered whether it was worth phoning back, to make the point that the lives of poets and scientific pioneers were not strictly comparable. He might mention, too, that being an unpublished (and therefore failed) poet was about twenty times more life-endangering than being (say) W.H. Auden, who rarely contended with stinging letters from *Caravan and Trailer* ('I read your poems with interest, Mr Auden, but I can't imagine why you sent them'). But he decided not to bother, and immediately cheered up. He would write an epic poem about rejection letters, simply for his own amusement. To say that writers are generally depressed, he reflected with satisfaction, is on a par with saying that Kentucky professors tell people precisely what they know already.

‿

I don't know what a reservoir dog is. I mean, I know that a new heist-movie called *Reservoir Dogs* has just opened, which is where the expression comes from; but after that my information runs out. Evidently the film is rather nasty but brilliant, is set in a warehouse after a failed robbery, and has a great central performance from Harvey Keitel. But curiously there are no dogs. And there is an infamous torture scene, and lots of blood, and fantastic suspense about which of the six conspirators tipped off the police. Yet the canine input, as such, is small. In short, then, nobody should buy a ticket under the illusion that *Reservoir Dogs* represents the relaunch of the animal picture. If the organizers of this week's Cruft's have bought it as a treat for the last day of the show, they should reconsider.

I raise this matter not just because I am irredeemably literal-minded, but because when the director of the film appeared on *Moving Pictures* (BBC2) he seemed to be saying that actually he didn't know what the title meant either. He just liked it, and when producers had frowned and tut-tutted, he had fobbed them off with a fancy answer about French gangland argot, which like prize mutts they had fallen for. Quentin Tarantino is his name, and this is his first film. He seemed young and over-excited, and was evidently a stranger to the benefits of personal grooming, but to say that he was wised up to the movie business would be like saying Edward Scissorhands was sharp. He knew perfectly well that a title like *Reservoir Dogs* raises images in people's minds, but no awkward questions. Also, that the moment it enters common parlance ('Seen *Reservoir Dogs* yet?'), it tucks itself into a nice safe corner of the memory where semantics does not intrude.

Obscure titles have one great advantage, of course: they flatter the punters. This explains why so many up-market book titles take allusions from other writers, or invoke the names of famous intellectuals. A little while ago there was a spate of titles so obviously following in the footsteps (or possibly claw-prints) of *Flaubert's Parrot* by Julian Barnes, that I began to suspect a directive had gone out from publishers, with the promise of a bag of nuts for the best entry: *Balzac's Horse, Schrödinger's Cat, Foucault's Pendulum, Aubrey's Raven, Kafka's Dick*. I remember vowing at the time that if I were ever to write a novel, I would hitch my skateboard to the bandwagon and plump for *Einstein's Tick*, or *Savonarola's Bum*, or *Darwin's Teapot*, and hang the consequences. It wouldn't matter that the book didn't fit the title, because obviously the allusion is so clever it doesn't have to. And if pushed, like the director of *Reservoir Dogs*, you could just make something up ('Darwin's teapot? Well, obviously, it stands for bone-china fragility in a tough survivalist world').

Mainly, however, you would rely on the fact that somewhere in the back of the collective mind there are philosophical things such as Occam's Razor, which sound fantastically difficult and all-encompassing and seriously paradoxical, and just right for a modern book. In the end, by the way, I pretty well settled on *Heidegger's Bactrian* for my own novel. It's a title that suggests all sorts of things, including two handy humps of water for emergencies. *Occam's Wash-Mitt* I will preserve for another occasion. And just to cover all the angles, I will give my book the full title of *Heidegger's Bactrian: Now a Major Motion Picture Starring Daniel Day-Lewis*.

Meanwhile it is slightly worrying to realize how unthinkingly all titles are assimilated in one's mind. No sooner have you heard of David Mamet's *Glengarry Glen Ross* than it becomes simply something to get your tongue round, not to ask damn-fool questions about. Recently I met a man who had seen *Pygmalion* at the National Theatre and who clearly had no idea where the title came from, but had not let this trouble him for an instant. Fair enough. Not everyone carries a *Larousse Classical Encyclopedia* in their coat pocket. As far as he was concerned, *Pygmalion* was the name of a famous play by George Bernard Shaw; why did it have to *mean* anything? Indeed, I just wish I'd said it was French gangland argot, or something, to see how far I would get.

Of course, it was probably just a silly little administrative over-sight, but I nevertheless yowled with agony when I realized I hadn't been invited to this year's Booker Prize. 'Will you be going to the dinner?' my nice literary holiday companions had asked, as we lay beside our swimming-pool in Italy, catching up on our Ian McEwans. 'Me?' I said carelessly. 'To the Booker Prize? On Tuesday 16 October at the Guildhall at 6.15 (drinks in the Old Library)? Oh, I shouldn't think so. Haven't really given it much thought.'

I don't suppose anyone was fooled by this rather obvious dissimulation. When I got home from holiday, I was so desperate to find out whether I had received an invitation that I screeched the car to a halt outside the house (leaving it blocking a bus-lane) and rushed inside to ransack every item of post that had arrived in my absence. The cats, who had not seen me for three weeks, looked distinctly pained as I paced up and down, distractedly shuffling envelopes and shouting four-letter words. But when at last I admitted defeat, and lay stunned on a heap of litter, they came and sat on my chest, and discreetly looked the other way.

Now, I know what you are asking. Why the fuss? It's something I can't explain. But if it is anything to do with pride, why did I phone the Booker Trust three days before the dinner and beg to be admitted? Their kind suggestion was that I could most certainly come to the Guildhall, but that unfortunately I might have to eat my meal in a different room from everyone else (the 'parlour') and watch the proceedings on a monitor. Sounds all right, I thought, I can live with that. Just so long as they don't single me out in any other way – like stamping 'ONE DRINK ONLY' on my forehead, or shouting 'You! Out!' if I attempted to strike up a conversation with Beryl Bainbridge in the toilets.

In the event, however, I didn't spend much time in the 'parlour', because a nice lady came along just after I had completed my first course and said that I could join the main event. 'Does it matter that I've eaten something?' I asked anxiously. It was quite disconcerting, actually, to be picked out for this honour, and conducted at a brisk pace from the rather cheerless parlour (which reminded me of being in a classroom at eight o'clock in the evening) to the glitz and hubbub of the grown-ups' dinner. Did I feel proud and exhilarated as we strode along? No; strangely, I was too desperate and anxious to feel either of these things. In fact, what kept coming into my head was an intensely paranoid recollection of an old Nazi trick I had seen in umpteen prisoner-of-war films. Perhaps the Booker people were only telling me I had been released from the parlour, so that – just as I broke into a run – they could shoot me in the back and use me as an example to others. 'Nobody,' they could say afterwards, 'invites herself to the Booker Prize and gets away with it.'

About a month ago, Alan Coren wrote a column on this page about the loss of his novel. Perhaps I should just phone him, but on the other hand I feel I am too distant a relative to intrude on the grief. The thing is, he said he had been writing this novel on the quiet, had fetched up 20,000 words of it, and then lost the whole damn lot when his computer in France was nicked. As it is well attested that a writer cannot possibly reconstruct the thing from memory, his novel-writing days were thus officially over, and it was no great tragedy. He was taking it surprisingly well.

Well, obviously one's chin wobbled a bit. A tear fell into one's Common Sense breakfast food. The man was so brave. The traditional lost manuscript (of which the lost hard disk is the modern equivalent) is a highly touching motif for anyone who has ever attempted a sustained piece of fiction. Our words are our children, you know. Remember the despair of Eilert Lovborg in *Hedda Gabler* when he realized he had thoughtlessly abandoned his infant manuscript in a whorehouse? How the words 'child murder' came up, and in his remorse he shuffled off into the dark Norwegian night with a revolver? I pictured the two gruff French burglars, both played by Arthur Mullard, breaking into Mr Coren's gaff and shining big rubber torches about. 'Vous êtes coming wiv us,' they said in deep voices, alighting on the computer. 'Non, non,' piped the novel, its eyes round with panic, 'Papa! Papa!' 'Har, har,' they laughed, 'Votre papa habeets en Cricklywood! Il est miles away.' And then they threw a black sack over its head before ... well, I can't go on.

But the reason I write this is that at the same time as feeling Lovborgian empathy with Mr Coren's loss, I also feel intensely envious. You mean, your novel has just *gone*? Just like that? How absolutely fantastic. Personally, I have reached the late laborious paranoid stage in my own creative outpouring when its unfinished state gnaws at me like a constant reproach, and its mewlings for attention drive me mad with guilt. Which is why, whenever someone innocently asks, 'How's the novel?' I actually feel like screaming, or pulling a gun. 'Novel?' I want to yell, waving the weapon in dangerous circles. 'Did you ask about my novel?' I fumble with the trigger, wildly push back my fringe, and take a swig from a bottle. 'What do you know about it? Just what do you think you know about it? You know nothing,' – I start to sob, here – 'Nothing, nothing ...' The outburst tails off. I drop the gun. I give myself up. It's all over.

People are only being nice, when they ask. To the enquirer, 'How's the novel?' is like saying 'How's your Mum?' – friendly, concerned, non-judgemental. All that's required by way of response is, 'Fine thanks, how's yours?' But unfortunately this simple question, when filtered through the cornered-animal mentality of the weary last-lap novelist, is transformed into the sort of sneering insinuation that makes homicide justifiable. 'It was peculiar,' friends say to one another, when I pop out of the room. 'All I said was "How's the novel?" and look, she bit my hand.' 'Tsk, tsk,' the others agree, shaking their heads and peeling back the fresh bandages on their own nicks and flayings. 'How did you get those bruised ribs again, Terry?' 'Well, we were at dinner, and she'd put down her knife and fork, and I said brightly, "Have you finished?" That's all. And she flew at me.'

They don't realize how sensitive you can get. They don't know what it's like to live constantly with this Tiny Tim of an unfinished book, sitting trusting and wistful in the inglenook of your consciousness waiting for you to fix its calipers and make it well. It's such a drag. My novel can do nothing independently; I can't pay somebody else to look after it in the afternoons; and if ultimately it gets botched, it will be nobody's fault but mine. So I keep thinking of Mr Coren's novel, kidnapped by ruffians, and considering whether, all in all, this unkind fate would not be preferable. 'How's the novel?' people would ask, automatically ducking sideways and shielding their faces with their arms. 'Oh, didn't I tell you?' I could say dolefully (as if sad). 'It's gone.' 'What?' 'Yes, I left it outside a supermarket, and just my luck, someone lured it away with a packet of crisps.'

~

The historical Saint Valentine was clubbed to death, you know. And now, seventeen centuries later, by means of one of those great arching ironies to which history is so partial, the rest of us are being clubbed to death by St Valentine's Day. We are bludgeoned with love, and I am not sure I like it. Formerly St Valentine's was one of those optional festivals, like Septuagesima, which you could celebrate at your own discretion. It was also, I always thought, associated with the finer, more delicate aspects of love: tremulous, unspoken, violet-scented. But a heavy hand in a red velvet glove has taken care of such love-heart nonsense, and St Valentine's has turned overnight into an excuse for relentless Channel 4 extravaganzas featuring wall-to-wall exhibitionism and rumpy-pumpy. A certain grossness, it must be said, has poked its way into the sweet satin folds of the romance, and 'Be my Valentine' is no longer a wistful request.

Isn't February depressing enough, without this? Channel 4 sent me a little bottle of massage oil in celebration of the 'Love Weekend' and I have been thinking seriously about drinking it. But leaving aside all the arguments on behalf of lonely stay-at-homes (and romantics) dismayed and alienated by frank, endless sex-talk on the telly, isn't it just spit-awful to find yet another date in the calendar turned irrevocably into an imperative national event, demanding special film seasons on the box? I mean, where will it end? It was actually a surprise, on Monday, to see the world return to normal, with the banks open, and people going off to work. 'No holiday, then?' I breathed in relief, thankful for the small mercy.

Personally, I am now dreading next week's Pancake Day, for fear that the TV channels will be given over to a 'Night of Batter'. I hardly dare open my *Radio Times*:

BBC2, 7.50pm: a short, irreverent history of the Jif lemon.

8pm: an in-depth profile of modern artists whose chosen medium is pancake-and-gouache.

Midnight until 4am: an acclaimed, sobering French movie about the unremembered crêperie wars that shook Paris during the Occupation.

Channel 4, meanwhile, could fill a studio with talentless ugly nude people with frying-pans on their heads, extracting endless nervous hilarity from the word 'toss'. It could all happen; I sincerely believe it. Something for everyone, that's the principle of these theme nights; only unfortunately it usually comes out curiously awry, as everything for someone.

I said I would leave aside the special-pleading arguments about lonely stay-at-homes struck downhearted and dismal by the excesses of this past weekend, but the pancake analogy somehow invites them back to the forefront again. Because – well, it's obvious. While for single people (and people not happily in love, which is a different category that includes nearly everyone) the whole dark, heaving Valentine event is so dispiriting it makes the depression of Christmas seem like a hayride to a clambake, Pancake Day requires no special personal circumstances for its enjoyment, and is therefore, actually, a better cause for celebration. Hm, I may be on to something. I mean, you don't have to be 'lurved' as a prerequisite for Pancake Day, just handy with a whisk. I have never thought of it this way before, but the pancake is obviously a great leveller. Old and young, ugly and beautiful, we can all roll them up and squirt them with lemons – and if we choose not to, it's not because there is anything wrong with us.

It is sad to think how St Valentine's is going – but on the other hand, the hell with it. You've got Shrove Tuesday to look forward to. Moreover, there is still time to record a short sequence on video describing your first pancake, your ideal pancake, your lost pancake, or the final pancake that left you feeling a bit sick and sorry for yourself. And the funny thing is, that compared with many of the dreary sexual relationships displayed and analysed on the 'Love Weekend', your pancakes will probably appear to have colour, individuality, interest – and above all, depth.

⌒

When Raoul Fitzgerald Hernandez O'Flaherty, the hot-blooded Irish-Argentinian international polo ace, called me up on Friday from his helicopter, begging me to join him on a weekend trip to Palm Beach, I admit I was slightly taken aback. This is a bit irregular, I thought. I had planned a nice weekend rearranging my dried fruit collection and mending my string bag, and now here was Randy Raoul hovering spectacularly over my front garden, showering emerald trinkets into my bird-bath, and demanding by loud-hailer that I go and inspect some new ponies.

Of course I became an expert on horse-flesh years ago, when I avidly consumed books such as *Jill Enjoys Her Ponies*. Also, I spent many childhood Sunday afternoons 'treading in' (stamping on divots) between chukkas at a nearby polo club. Yet I had a strange feeling that it was my body, not my equine expertise, that Raoul was really after. The O'Flaherty triplets are all notorious wom-anizers, but Raoul is the best lover of the three, ranked number eight in the world! Raoul clearly wanted to pluck me from my flat, lavish all sorts of sexual attention on me, drive me wild with jewels and frocks, and drop hilarious innuendoes about the thrill of goal-scoring. What on earth was a girl to do?

Well, the string bag is much better now, you will be relieved to hear. The currants are tucked in neatly behind the prunes. But I am seriously wondering what to do with this copy of Jilly Cooper's *Polo*, which seems to be the source of the trouble. What do other women do in these circumstances? As a mere novice to the so-called bonk-buster novel (obliged to read *Polo* for purely professional reasons) I had no idea it would fill my world with rich, good-looking blokes with strong brown arms akimbo. I poke through my jewellery and can't believe my eyes. What, no perfect emeralds, gift of an infatuated millionaire? No diamonds? How can it be true that my only ring is the one I bought for a fiver in a place called Mousehole? Thank goodness the Freudian heyday is a thing of the past.

Of course I am not the ideal reader for a bonk-buster novel, because I am not married. I am free to get excited in the polo tournament bits ('Come on, you brave little ponies!') and to salivate openly during the sex scenes, whereas the target reader will be a married woman on a beach somewhere, obliged to disguise her reactions for the benefit of the husband (not rich, not handsome, and can't tell a divot from a hole in the ground). While reading, she controls her breathing, tries not to perspire too visibly, and occasionally breaks off during a particularly juicy bit to say offhandedly 'Not very good, this, actually', before plunging back again and memorizing the page number for later on.

For me personally, on the other hand, *Polo* recalled all those *Jill and Her Ponies* books I used to read when I was ten. Who will win the silver cup? Will the pony rescued from cruelty turn into the best little pony in the world? This jolly gymkhana stuff made me feel quite young again, but it also made me wonder whether the Jill in question grew up to become Jilly in later life. It is not impossible. After all, the fictional Jill's mother was a writer – but an unsuccessful one who clearly overlooked the bankable nature of her own daughter's pony-mad activities. Poor Jill was obliged to wear second-hand jodhpurs to the Pony Club Gymkhana, which is just the sort of indignity (in bonk-busters, anyway) that makes an ambitious girl grow up aching for a shot at some serious dosh.

I am not sure, in retrospect, that we were supposed to despise Jill's mum for being a hopeless breadwinner. In fact, I used to think it was sweet that when the pig-tailed Jill came home on summer afternoons – all dusty from a hack on Black Boy, all worried about where the next curry-comb was coming from – there would be Mother, leaning out of the window of their little cottage, excitedly waving a small piece of paper. 'A cheque!' she would yell. 'I've sold a story in London!' And my heart would leap. 'Saddle up Black Boy again, Jill,' Mother would say. 'Today we'll have buns for tea!'

Such innocence. It makes you feel all old and jaded and peculiar. True, I always shout 'Buns for tea!' when a cheque arrives in the post, but it is heavily ironic, since I know perfectly well that the money will only service the overdraft, or go half-way towards some car insurance (buns doesn't come into it). But I prefer the world of 'Buns for tea!' to the casual purchase of Renoirs and Ferraris to be found in *Polo*. Cream puffs evidently mean nothing on the international polo circuit; teacakes make them laugh.

I think this is why, in the end, I turned down Raoul's tempting offer of the Palm Beach trip. So what, if these polo people are good at jewels and orgasms, if they are blind to the value of an honest barm cake? Of course, memory may be playing tricks here: perhaps Jill and her mum sang 'Diamonds Are a Girl's Best Friend' in the evenings, while flipping through glossy magazines for pictures of rich people. Perhaps they would have killed for a chance to fly off to the world of Cartier and great sex, leaving the second-hand jodhpurs in a heap on the ground. In which case, when Raoul O'Flaherty came to call, perhaps I made a rather large mistake.

A few years ago, I met a dynamic woman journalist who told me she was keen to launch a new daily paper aimed at a female readership. Unfortunately for the ensuing discourse, our meeting took place at the wrong end of a highly boozy book-award dinner, at that delirious point in the evening when you start to pass out in your chair, and think hey, that's nice, everyone's a bunny rabbit. So when this charismatic woman mentioned the newspaper idea, I couldn't think how to react, except with boundless enthusiasm. 'Great,' I shouted, so loudly that other people looked round. 'Brilliant, I mean, brilliant,' I added, in a whisper, and knocked back another glass of port as if to show how brilliant I thought it really was. 'Er, how would it be different exactly? What would you put in?' 'Well, the main thing is this,' she said. 'It's what you *take out*.' I smiled in a vague what's-she-talking-about kind of way and concentrated for a couple of minutes on trying to rest my chin on my hand, without success. 'All right, what do you take out?' I slurred at last, leaning forward. 'You take out the sport,' she said.

I never saw this woman again, but I often think of her. Until I met her, I would never have dared to assert that sport was uninteresting to all (or most) women; I just thought I had a blind spot. But now, when I open my *Times* in the morning, flipping the second section adroitly into the bin (only to rescue it later with a stifled scream and a flurry of soggy tea-bags when I remember the arts pages), I know I am not alone. Similarly, when the *Today* programme reaches twenty-five past the hour ('Now, time for sport') and I rush about for precisely five minutes doing the noisy jobs such as bath-running and kettle-boiling, I am confident that countless other people are doing the same. And finally, when a programme such as *Sports Review of the Year* soaks up two hours of BBC1 peak-time on a Sunday night, I happily regard it as a gap in the schedule, and read a book. Fran Lebowitz spoke for me and for millions, I quite believe, when she said the only thing she had in common with sports fanatics was the right to trial by jury.

I mention all this because on Sunday I eschewed the usual literary treat and forced myself to watch *Sports Review* instead. I had heard about the time-honoured award for BBC Sports Personality of the Year, and envisaged it as a bit of a laugh, with household-name sports heroes lined up in swimsuits and sashes ('Mister Cricket', 'Mister 100 Metres' and so on) trying to impress Desmond Lynam with their breadth of hobbies and love of travel, and nervously pushing back their tiaras as they paraded at the end. Of course, it turned out to be much less interesting than that, with lots of unidentifiable sports people got up like funeral directors, but it did conclude quite as oddly, when Nigel Mansell (the winner, a racing driver) addressed the viewer at home and said that he would like to thank us all for supporting him.

For a moment he was so convincing that I almost didn't notice. 'Any time, Nige. Don't mention it, old son,' I said, wiping a tear. But then I remembered that I never watch racing driving (can't stand the *nyow-nyow*; can't stomach the commentators; can't follow who's winning; hate the bit when they squirt champagne). And it suddenly occurred to me: These people don't know. They really don't know that sport is a minority interest. When they say 'England' and assume you will understand a team of footballers, they forget completely that the word has another (if only a secondary) meaning. Far be it from me to argue that other people should not enjoy sport. It is merely childish to argue against something on the grounds that you don't know what they see in it. I just wish to point out, for those who didn't know, that in a large number of households the television news gets switched off automati-

cally when the announcer says, 'Cricket, and at Edgbaston ...'
And also that sometimes, when drunk and in the pleasant
company of the cast of *Watership Down*, one can believe for a
bright shining moment that the collective indifference is so
very marked, it might even be marketable.

⁓

How heartening to know that the prime minister buys books
he doesn't have time to read. No piece of news has ever, metaphorically speaking, drawn him closer to my bosom. I doubt it
was meant to, however. The thought of him excitedly shuffling
his book tokens at Waterstone's check-out has already elicited
sneers – intellectual snobs being always alert for vulgarians
proudly displaying their embossed Shakespeare with the disclaimer, 'Of course, it's not something you can actually read'.
But personally, I take great comfort in the news; it gives him a
whole new human side. He has faith in the future. At the same
time, he sensibly realizes that busy jobs don't last for ever. He
likes books for their own sake. And when people look at his
shelves and say, 'Have you read all these?', he replies without
embarrassment, 'No, but I live in hope.'

My own sensitivity on this issue I can trace to my days as
a guilty, hard-pressed literary editor in an office waist-deep
with neglected review copies. 'Have you read all these?' people
would enquire, innocuously enough, and then draw back in
alarm as I scrambled to the window ledge and threatened to
jump. They learnt not to ask. At home, I own literally hundreds
of books I have bought, but not yet read; but if I say I regard
them as a squirrel regards his nuts, I hope you will pardon the
expression and catch my drift. I mean, what is the point of
owning only books you *have* read? Where is the challenge or
excitement in that? It would be like having a fridge full of food
you have already eaten, cupboards of booze that's already been

drunk. Imagine browsing for a meal in the evenings – 'Mm, this moussaka was pretty good last time, and I reckon Mister Retsina could stand another paddle down the old alimentary canal.'

Of course, I have made mistakes, bought books I couldn't get on with. By rights, I should donate them to passing students, but instead I hoard them, like ill-fitting shoes, in hope that one day I will make the effort to break them in. Henry James is no good at all, God knows I've tried, but from the very first sentence I always find myself sinking, disappearing, drowning in dark mud, it's horrible, horrible, and finally I cry out in Thurberesque despair, 'Why doesn't somebody take this damn thing away from me?' Yet if I retain my copy of The Golden Bowl, it's not because I am dishonestly feigning an abiding love of Henry James, it's just because I like to be prepared for all contingencies. Who knows, but one day I may positively yearn for intellectual suffocation in mud? Similarly, who knows, but I might break a leg and catch up on all my Gary Larson 'Far Side' books as well.

No, I defend the prime minister's position. First, I think there is a moral imperative to buy books, even if you have little time to read them. After all, the authors wrote them in all good faith; why should they be penalized just because you are busy (temporarily) running the country? I grow very cross in bookshops, watching customers dither over fulfilling their obligation. 'Just buy it, for heaven's sake!' I want to say. 'What's the big deal? First Lord of the Treasury salary not good enough for you?' Second, there is no pleasure to compare with a heavy Waterstone's bag. And third (obviously), if you wait for the exact appropriate moment to buy the exact appropriate book, it will no longer be in print, stupid.

I keep trying to imagine the sort of person whose bookshelves don't say 'This is what I'm interested in' but 'This is what I've read, actually; go on, test me.' What a miserable way to live your life. I remember once a potential boyfriend (it came to nothing) solemnly inspecting my bookshelves as though they were a measure of compatibility, and I thought, lumme, he'll ask about those German poets, I'm done for. But then he leaned back and said, 'I see you've got M.R. James, Henry James and P.D. James all together here.' 'Er, is there a problem?' I said, nervously. 'Well, yes,' he snapped. 'Alphabetically, Henry should come before M.R. Also, the books should be drawn forward neatly to the extreme edge of the shelves.' It took me several weeks to realize it, but this reaction said more about him than it did about me.

If M.R. James or Sheridan Le Fanu were alive today, I have no doubt about the particular universal neurosis they would be tapping – terrifying us out of our skins by making a simple story out of our deepest nightmare. The story they would be writing would be called 'The Newspaper'.

On the staircase of the London Library in St James's Square, a middle-aged clergyman (his hair prematurely white) would meet by chance a young man with whom he had once shared a railway compartment on a journey to York. After a few pleasantries, they would decide to take tea together, perhaps in Fortnum's. Only when they had seated themselves comfortably in a quiet corner with some Darjeeling and some dry cake would the clergyman relate – in simple, unsensational prose – his terrible story.

On a summer morning in the year of 198—, he had bought, he says, a Sunday newspaper. After scanning it for church news, he had left it in his conservatory while he pottered peacefully among his roses, stopping occasionally to make a fuss of Theo, his faithful old Labrador. Returning once to the conservatory for an implement – a trowel, let's say – he had sensed something odd; something not quite as he had left it. But glancing around, he had seen nothing particularly out of the ordinary: perhaps the newspaper, with his spectacles resting on it, had shifted slightly – but no doubt, he reasoned, Theo had been sniffing about. He thought little more of it, and later shut the conservatory door and strolled up the lane to his pretty parish church for Evensong.

Returning later, he thought he heard the dog whimpering. The sound was one he had never heard from Theo before – *deep fear was there in that sound*. The clergyman, his pulse racing, frantically searched the house for his faithful friend, but only when Theo started to yowl and scratch furiously at the door did he realize that the sound was coming from the conservatory. Tearing open the door, he saw the most terrible sight: the dog, frothing at the mouth, was lying on its side, its red eyes starting out of its head, its old heart having given out at last. And in the corner, the Newspaper, no longer an inoffensive two-section broadsheet, but now an indescribably huge, ugly, monstrous, garish, unnecessary object. In the course of a single day, the Newspaper had grown exponentially, in that poor clergyman's conservatory, to *one hundred times its original size*.

The terror of that moment still seized the clergyman, even in the safety of the tea-room. During their modest repast, his fine bone china teacup rattled and danced on its saucer, and though he broke his madeira cake into pieces, never did he raise a morsel to his lips. The *Sunday Times* had done for him. It has done for us all.

Personally I would be sorry to see it go, that nice busy roundabout outside Buckingham Palace. Last week's news that the Royal Parks Review Group wants to pedestrianize it for the sake of tourists has come as a blow. Naturally, I can't fault their humanitarian motives, indeed I can easily picture the escalating woe their research must have induced, as, faces fixed in a rictus of alarm, they kept their St James's Park vigil, and monitored the near-hits with a regular muffled shriek. 'I can't look!' they squealed, as every ten minutes a clueless foreign tourist, intent on the Palace, ventured halfway across the road from the Victoria Memorial, stopped, blinked for a moment, panicked, flapped his arms, and then at the very last minute vaulted the crash-barrier out of the path of a roaring cab.

But why don't they look at it from the other point of view? For the average Londoner, this game of high-speed chicken outside a national heritage beauty-spot is one of our very few opportunities to contribute usefully to the tourist industry. It's our only chance to interact. And it is to our credit, I think, that we do it with such enthusiasm. 'There's one!' we say, dropping down a gear as we sweep round the corner from Birdcage Walk, and accelerate hard. 'This will give them something to write home about!' And quite honestly, the tourists do seem to appreciate it, especially when we make jolly local hand-gestures at them through the windscreens and shout 'Yah, turkeys!' as we thunder past. Safely arrived at the railings, they giggle red-faced from the chase, pant with pleasure, and sometimes even clutch their chestal area as testimony to the excitement. Which means that the gratified motorist can speed off up Constitution Hill to Hyde Park Corner with the pleasant satisfaction of a job well done.

Pave it over, make a namby-pamby promenade, and this precious interaction will most certainly be lost. But not only that; it will also give tourists the wrong impression of our lovely city, in which dangerous jay-walking is surely one of the chief means of expressing individuality and free will. 'I am going to cross this road *now*, though hell should bar the way!' we declare stoutly, as we stride out into four lanes of traffic, misjudge the speed of an oncoming motorbike, and pretend not to hear what's shouted at us as it swerves and skids to a halt at the lights, just twenty yards down the road. Traffic dodging is part of the metropolitan experience, for goodness' sake, it's part of being British.

What's the point of coming to London if you never expose yourself to the fear of being run over? You might as well stay at home and knit fjords, or whatever it is that foreigners do. Our high pedestrian accident rate should be made a glowing feature of tourism campaigns, not swept under the carpet. Look at it in a positive light, and these foreigners are returning to their homes equipped with a life skill they could not possibly acquire anywhere else outside the Third World.

No, if London's tourists deserve sympathy, it's for other things. The place is expensive and unfriendly, you can't get a coffee after half past five, London airport is curiously nowhere near London, and as for linguistic proficiency, well, let's just say our spoken English needs work. But since we don't make strenuous efforts to protect our honoured visitors from anything else in this hostile, uncomfortable culture, it is definitely a bit peculiar to want to save them from the cars. I mean, good grief, let's not get xenophobic here, but they do *make* these cars, you know. We only buy them and then drive in a reckless manner, as God intended.

So let's stop pussyfooting around. Leave that roundabout precisely where it is, with the traffic going clockwise to confuse the foreigners. After all, it could well be true that for every Japanese or German car squealing round and round the Victoria Memorial, sufficient funds flow back into the Japanese or German national kitty for several lucky people to pack a suitcase, fly to London, run across the road outside Buckingham Palace, and be almost knocked down. And if that's not a circular irony, then I don't know what is.

Should you ever feel the urge to see where Jim Morrison is buried (Jim Morrison of the Doors, d. 1971), I now feel pretty confident I can guide you to the spot. Prior to last weekend, I had only the vaguest idea that Morrison was interred somewhere in France; but now, having navigated a friend around the famous Parisian cemetery of Père-Lachaise ('Next stop Balzac, this way, step along'), I am an authority on Morrison's precise whereabouts, despite having no personal interest in him whatsoever. People just kept asking us, that's all, because we had a map. 'Jim Morrison?' they enquired earnestly, these young Italian girls with rucksacks and brown legs, born circa 1975. 'Er, oh yes, down here, turn right, follow the crowd,' we said, mystified.

It seemed a bit peculiar, all this fuss. My friend and I appeared to be missing the point of Père-Lachaise, getting excited about Rossini and Colette, when we obviously should have been focusing our dilated eyeballs to scrawl, 'We miss you JIM, where are you JIM, are you dead then JIM' on the side of somebody else's tomb abutting the mighty Morrison's. What terrible luck for those bourgeois Parisian families, incidentally, who found themselves slap-bang next to a blown-out Sixties youth icon. No chance of resting in peace. An American couple asked us near the gate who was buried in Père-Lachaise. 'Who isn't?' we exclaimed, jabbing wildly at our map. 'No, look, Proust, Bizet, Géricault' (no response); 'Er, Chopin, Modigliani, Oscar Wilde, Edith Piaf, Jim Morrison –' 'Really? Jim Morrison?' they interrupted. And they went off happy. We could see they were impressed.

But as we continued our tour of this starry necropolis, sadly taking note of the fact that devotees of *A la Recherche* had failed to write, 'I can't live without you MARCEL, Come back MARCEL, This is what happens when you go out MARCEL' on the grave of Proust, I suppose we should have realized that Jim Morrison, for all his paucity of talent or achievement, really is the point of Père-Lachaise. What does it matter that Proust is here? He is only where he ought to be. In any cemetery, the deepest sentiment is rightly reserved for the exile or itinerant who happened to step on a bee in an unlikely place, and got buried before anyone noticed. For the best effect, Proust should be in Florida. 'No no MARCEL' we would write. 'Whatever possessed you MARCEL.'

I speak as someone who has wept openly at the Keats-Shelley memorial in Rome, has stood bereft at the tomb of Henry Fielding in Lisbon, but who visits Poets' Corner in Westminster Abbey dry-eyed and impervious. It is the sorry truth: the sight of a hero properly interred in his own country is rarely an occasion for a Kleenex, whereas the idea of poor Fielding, one of England's greatest (and most English) writers, embarking for Lisbon in 1754, arriving there, loathing it, and dying in just a few weeks, is somehow heartbreaking. Furthermore, it adds to the touching romance of the thing that his monument is nowadays difficult to find. I remember asking a bemused Portuguese leaf-sweeper for directions, and he clearly had no idea what I was driving at – even when I helpfully mimed scenes from the movie of *Tom Jones*.

All this has been much on my mind because, two or three weeks from now, I hope to stand on a hilltop in Western Samoa looking at the tomb of Robert Louis Stevenson, on which his famous 'Requiem' is engraved.

> Under the wide and starry sky
> Dig the grave and let me lie,
> Glad did I live and gladly die,
> And I laid me down with a will.

And, well, pardon me for sniffing, I must have a cold coming on, but why does nobody understand that this is intensely moving? They understand about Jim Morrison, but 'Stevenson?' they say, 'I don't get it. Surely he invented the *Rocket* and that was that.' Clearly I've got a big job ahead of me, scrawling, 'All right LOUIS, It's your centenary soon LOUIS, They are hoping to do a commemorative stamp LOUIS.' But it really shouldn't be necessary, when the poem says it all:

> This be the verse you grave for me,
> Here he lies where he longed to be,
> Home is the sailor, home from sea,
> And the hunter home from the hill.

I bet JIM wishes he'd thought of that.

Crackers Already

If the build-up to Christmas is depressing for no other reason, it is because Ambridge is annually gripped by showbiz fever. Rural readers will no doubt assure me that English village life in Advent really is abuzz with pantomime rehearsals and sheet-music distribution, and I suppose I will have to believe it. But the thought of Jill Archer efficiently running up yet another dozen chorus-line costumes on her Singer treadle, of Bert Fry practising his basso profundo in the byre, of Linda Snell bustling importantly with clipboard and Tiggy-whistle, makes me shake my head with genuine sadness. There are several reasons. First, it is essentially the same story every time (although this year, admittedly, the panto has been cancelled in favour of the even duller concert); second, the annual repetition reminds me of my own mortality; third, I don't believe in this universal urge to leap on stage in a funny suit; and fourth, it gives me the shuddering Christmassy ab-dabs to think of the lights going up after the show each year to reveal a silent audience of – what?

Much has been made of the popular 'unheard' characters in *The Archers* – such people as Higgs, Shane and Pru Forrest, who neatly contrive to pop out suddenly ('He was here a minute ago –') to check the Bentley, the quiche, or the victoria sponge, and so avoid contact with the listening public. But only at Christmas does one become powerfully aware of the Ambridge plebs – that mob of mute, unnamed, disenfranchised villagers who must surely constitute the bums on seats for each miserably jolly extravaganza the Ambridge nobs can dream up for their delectation. *Who are they, these faceless inferiors? What does it feel like to be valued only for one's bum?* The rest of the year, they patronize the village shop, use the services of the doctor and vet, buy pints of Shires in the Bull, and take early morning swims at the Grey Gables health club – and presumably don't feel particularly second-class or invisible. But at Christmas, as they shuffle into that village hall, sit down and open their programmes, their wraith-like howls of bitter dismay must be audible all the way to Borchester.

I was put in mind of these non-people when reading yesterday of the nine-year-old Shetland schoolgirl whose mother is keeping her at home because of a disagreement with the head teacher. Nothing remarkable in that, you might think, until you discover that the girl (poor thing) is the real-life equivalent of the Ambridge nobs. If this school has a panto, she stars in it automatically. If it has a hockey team, she is its captain and goalie. And if there is a maths test she sets the standard. She is, in short, the only child at the school; and no wonder she is having problems. Other children can stand at the back when netball teams are picked; they can bend down and tie up their shoelaces. Not this girl. For her, there is no hiding place; she is forever in the spotlight. And every time the English teacher says, 'Now who's going to read aloud this morning?', she is obliged resignedly to raise her hand, otherwise the whole pedagogic caboodle crumbles instantly to dust. On speech day, when she wins all the prizes but nobody claps, she must dearly wish for another life.

Where the intense weirdness comes in, however, is that initially she was sent home for misbehaviour – a very strange case of *pour encourager les autres*. Sometimes she must dream of classmates – of skipping while other people turn the rope, of marble games in which you lose the yellow one and go home crying, of rough children pushing you into a hedge for no reason – just as Phil Archer must sometimes think that in a place like Ambridge there must be some other muggins who can play the joanna. But at least she knows that having been sent home, she is not the subject of a whispering campaign. One just wonders whether her head teacher, having evidently lost his patience with the girl and said, 'You! Trouble-maker! Out!', really felt much better when she'd obeyed, shrugged and gone home. Is the school running more smoothly now? Do the nativity play rehearsals progress without incident? In this Shetland school, as in Ambridge, I suspect you may eavesdrop on the festivities this year, and hear the famous eerie sound of one hand clapping.

⸙

The announcement of the Princess of Wales's controversial Christmas holiday plans contained an important sub-text, I thought, which somehow got ignored in the usual flurry of pecking and stripping to the bone when the vultures descended. 'You are blind!' I shouted at nobody in particular, as I pawed through my heap of tabloids. I mean, of course, yes, Diana's decision to spend Christmas away from the royal in-laws has 'fuelled speculation' (yawn). And yes, too, it has encouraged sentimental visions of Christmas Future at Sandringham, with the royal family casting sad-eyed Cratchit-like glances at the forlorn little wooden stool on which the princess formerly sat. But in the rush for that 4-star speculation-fuel, nobody noticed that in terms of universal yuletide family politics, Diana had achieved a tremendous coup. She had really caught them on the hop. To announce your Christmas plans in the first week of November is the mark of a brilliant tactician, family-wise. They can't possibly have been prepared for it. What she did was the equivalent of winning the race while her competitors were still indoors lacing up their plimsolls.

Christmas is an awful thing, in my book. Ding Dong Merrily has little to do with it; and there is a limit to the number of times you can pretend not to know the ending of *Superman II*. Sometimes I sit back and imagine that Christmas will really be cancelled this year, and the idea fills me with excitement. So I envy the princess her determined effort to avoid the tidal pull of the family Christmas, and I would emulate her like a shot ('Off to Morocco, sorry!') if I did not suffer currently from 'denial'. You know that you can be 'in denial' about bereavement or alcoholism? Well, I have a theory that you can also be 'in denial' about Christmas, which makes it ultimately more dangerous.

Denial lasts a long, long time. You can recognize people in denial because we stand aghast in department stores and scoff loudly, 'Hell's bells, not crackers already!' (leaving other shoppers to interpret this outburst as they will). Out of every magazine you pick up, there slithers a heavy catalogue of ingenious Christmas gifts, which you stare at uncomprehendingly. What's this, you say; a pair of slippers with headlights built in? If this is Christmas, you declare, you will have no part of it.

But mixed with this denial is guilt, of course, because one can't help noticing that other people have 'started'. It is somehow awful to hear.

'Have you started yet?' they say, sort-of casually.

'No, it's only November. Ha ha. You?'

'Mmm. Three weeks ago.'

'Oh.'

Meanwhile relations start mentioning casually on the phone the lovely present they bought you while on holiday in July, the news of which makes you feel strangely weightless.

Presumably there are people in the world on whom this sort of moral blackmail makes no impression, but personally I allow it to flood me with feelings of inadequacy, year after year. And this, I might add, despite my certain knowledge, borne of dismally consistent experience, that the much- vaunted holiday present will turn out on Christmas morning to be a small box of fudge or a red plastic ball-point with my name on it.

Anyway, to return to the theory of stages, this powerful guilt phase finally propels you into an eruption of frantic activity, then a brief spell of euphoria, closely followed by let-down, anger, and finally blank exhaustion. And that's it. Another consumer Christmas, another absolutely pointless exercise, which you knew you didn't want to get involved in from the start. This is what I hate about Christmas, that while I object to it very loudly, and can see with painful clarity that it is a form of mass hysteria, I always end up participating anyway, and going the whole hog. We all do. Any form of protest – principled refusal to buy cheese footballs, for example – is feeble and simply makes you look mean.

The idea, therefore, of the princess stating her intentions so clearly and forcibly in regard to the Sandringham three-line whip is really quite inspiring. Based on no evidence whatsoever, I shall assume, too, that when her Aunt Margaret pops her coat on and announces her intention of getting 'started', Diana will snap, 'Well, just don't get me a box of fudge like last year' – something I have always wanted to say, Diana, but fear I never shall.

Go on, guess. What's this? *Jing, jing, jing, jing-jing-jingaling, jing-jing-a-jing-aling-jing. Dee dee da, lovely weather for a sleigh ride together la laaah.*

Gosh, that's better. When a girl has spent three solid

weekends at home poring over those special goody-crammed Christmas gift catalogues, she fancies she feels the sting of snow on her face, smells the rich vinyl on the Perry Como records, hears sleighbells on the roof, and remembers the exact weight, shape and fragrance of a tub of Lily of the Valley talcum powder unwrapped on Christmas morn. Oh yes.

In short, she is almost clinically depressed. 'Who wants all this stuff?' she wails, disconsolately flipping the gaudy, fun-packed pages. She looks back on her life and sees a great endless Jacob Marley charm bracelet made up of all the unwanted Christmas presents she has misguidedly given since the age of six.

'It still goes on,' she groans, flapping a catalogue from Boots or Debenhams. 'Oh yes, they even – and I hardly believe it – still have a section called "For Him".'

It is only at Christmas that I feel genuinely sorry for men. They get a terrible deal, and these catalogues are testimony to life's dreadful gender unfairness. From being an ordinary individual – albeit a moron, genius, couch potato, whatever – a man at Christmas becomes in his family's festively fevered mind an entirely notional 'For Him' entity who revels implausibly in manicure sets and backgammon boards and special golf-motif alarm clocks.

For men, Christmas morning is a very mystifying time, requiring an almost saintly selfless pretence. 'Oh look, a jigsaw depicting a huge plate of baked beans. How er, lovely. Ha, ha, that should keep me busy.' It is a very curious thing. Forbidden to buy socks and hankies, I once bought my father a beautiful leather-and-silver-plate hip flask and fully expected him to be stunned with gratitude, regardless of the significant fact that he never (ever) drank.

But as Susan Carter so rightly whined in a recent episode of *The Archers*, 'Men are so difficult to buy for.' Which is why, as a sort of punishment presumably, they get landed with travel shoe-care kits, novelty calculators, tiddly-cricket and Brut aftershave. 'Well, you're just too difficult to buy for' is the bristling sub-text of each gift, especially when thrust upon a man who:

a) wears trainers, and never goes anywhere;
b) has a calculator already;
c) has never played a parlour game in his life; and
d) has sported a large bushy beard for the past twenty years.

Being currently mateless, I feel I can expand on this topic without hurting anyone's feelings. So why are 'men' so difficult to buy for? Well, let us take Susan Carter's husband Neil as an example, and apply the usual mental processes by which a thoughtful gift-buyer selects a winner.

What makes Neil happy?
Um, ooh. Well, um. Pigs?
Let's try another angle. What does Neil aspire to?
Hmm, no, sorry, this is trickier than I thought.
All right, for heaven's sake, does he already have an alarm clock disguised as a miniature old-fashioned petrol pump, or a jigsaw depicting an enormous plate of baked beans?

I am not saying that all men are Neil Carter. If they were, the world would be full of pig farms, and we shouldn't be able to move for co-op feed orders. Perhaps I am just trying to justify my strange decision, last year, to buy a dear (male) friend a gaily printed cotton bandanna (the sort cowboys wear over their noses on dusty cattle-drives), accompanied by a dandy booklet entitled *Thirty-Five Things to do with a Bandanna*. My only excuse is that it just seemed like the ultimate male Christmas gift.

My friend could try it on, read about it, and puzzle very deeply over my reasons for giving it to him. And then afterwards, utterly stumped, he could put it in a drawer and wonder.

⌒

Christmas in our house starts on Christmas Eve with the ritual of the food blender. Once a year, I like to trot down to the shed to pull it out from under the lawnmower, blow off the grass and spiders, look at the blade to make sure it's clean, and then begin – whipping together my special recipe of Paxo stuffing, cherry mincemeat, Bailey's Irish Cream, chicken fat, Warninck's Avocaat, cobwebs, After Eight Mints and Bisto (to taste). When blended together in the right proportions, it looks a bit like cat vomit, but it makes a terrific all-purpose Christmas sauce, which can transform even your slimmer's meal of cottage cheese with prawns into a festive occasion. It also means that you always have something suitable in the fridge for dealing with those unexpected visitors on Boxing Day. (They won't trouble you again.)

On Christmas Day after lunch, I like the whole family to gather around the fire and play word-games. Which is a shame, because a) I don't have a fire; and b) everybody except me is a cat. The gratification of being able to beat a cat at Scrabble palled after the first couple of Christmases, and I wasn't sorry to throw in the towel. In any case, he always wanted to check everything in the dictionary, and it took *forever*. So now we play more simple party games. They hide the remote control for the TV, and I look for it; or they pretend that they didn't buy me anything again this year, and I pretend to believe them; or they vomit their Turkey Whiskas with Surprise Christmas Sauce, and I have to guess which bowl holds the uneaten dinner, and which the regurgitated.

We like to watch the TV on Christmas Day. Which is all right, because I've got one of those. As in every family, there are the usual fights over which channel it's going to be. I have already settled with them that we will tune in to *Back to the Future* on Christmas Day, but I'm a bit worried that they won't be able to follow it, and that I'll have to spend so much time explaining bits that have just happened that I will miss the next bits. (Just like the time we all watched *It's a Wonderful Life*.)

On Christmas Night I like to reflect on life. What is life like? Life is like hoping for a racing bike for Christmas, and getting a Spirograph. Life is like starting a painting-by-numbers in a great fit of enthusiasm and then realizing that the little pot of blue will never be enough for the great expanse of sky, and that you should have thinned it out when you started. Life is like being given a dart-board, then being told there's nowhere in the house that you can play darts. Life is like chewing your Christmas pudding really carefully because you are fearful you may be the lucky one with the threepenny bit.

That's what I like to do at Christmas.

The Arnolds Feign Death Until the Wagners, Sensing Awkwardness, are Compelled to Leave ...

A couple of weeks ago, on Radio 4's *In the Psychiatrist's Chair*, the late great Les Dawson confessed to a fault he had never been able to cure. 'What do you like least about yourself?' asked Anthony Clare (as he often does). That I can't say no to people, said Dawson; that I want to please them and, worst of all, that I'm never the person at the pub who just looks at his watch and decides it's time to go home. Bless you, Les Dawson, I thought. In a generally sympathetic interview, this admission was surely the most endearing moment of all.

As someone who has blithely waved away the last guests at other people's dinners, gamely collected glasses and turned off lights at other people's office parties, said 'Gosh, that's kind' to the fifth weary offer of coffee from hosts stapling their eyelids to their foreheads and propping their chins on broom-handles, I felt I knew precisely what he meant. Sometimes I worry that I live inside a Gary Larson cartoon, the one that's captioned: 'The Arnolds feign death until the Wagners, sensing awkwardness, are compelled to leave.'

Why does this awkwardness arise? No doubt the non-suffering majority (those decisive watch-glancers, coat-grabbers and leave-takers) think that we dreary obtuse Wagners refuse to collect our hats because we fear that people will talk about us. But it's nothing so simple. No, in fact we just feel that saying goodbye admits a failure to bond, and we can't stand it. I remember once interviewing Stephen Fry for a Sunday newspaper, spending two or three pleasant and fruitful hours in a Soho restaurant with him and then – on the pavement outside – finding myself completely unable to say 'Westward ho!' and strike off in a different direction, because I felt it would ruin everything.

'Well, I'm going this way,' he said, courteously offering his hand and wishing me luck. 'Oh, that's lucky, I can go that way!' I exclaimed nerdishly, utterly deaf to my cue. We walked towards Shaftesbury Avenue, where by chance he spied a 19 bus. 'I believe this will take me to Islington,' he said, jumping aboard and waving. 'Great idea,' I agreed, and jumped on, too. (It gives me no pleasure to recount this, believe me.) 'Do you know, I think I'll go *upstairs*,' he said, in a courteous last-ditch attempt to lose me, as we turned left at Cambridge Circus and sped up Charing Cross Road. At which point (outside Foyles) I finally realized it was time to say goodbye.

I disembarked, spent half an hour in a bookshop, and thought no more about it until I re-emerged and saw to my alarm that he was studying the window opposite. Clearly the long-suffering chap had likewise got off the bus immediately I was out of sight.

I often call to mind this excruciating memory when interviewers record their meetings with celebrities entirely in a manner to flatter themselves, registering every 'um' and 'er' of the responses while somehow forgetting to mention that there is another side to the story: that their own questions were offensive or ill-informed, or that they suddenly suffered a copious nosebleed just at the moment when the tape-recorder unspooled yards of tape which became entangled with the dog. I think with fondness of the actor Brian Cox, who patiently allowed me to interview him twice, because on the first occasion my tape-recorder silently self-combusted on his dressing-room sofa (leaving a hole). But mainly I think of those poor blighters – playwrights, directors, actors – who politely talked for several hours, until it finally (and horribly) dawned on them that 'enough's enough' was an expression which, despite being in English, held no meaning for me whatsoever.

Why isn't there therapy for this condition? After all, it would be incredibly simple to organize. Just get a group of fellow-sufferers together in a big room and then, well, make us all go home again. Fiddling with one's travelcard or car-keys while making vague dithery 'Gosh, is that the time?' noises would be strictly forbidden unless properly 'followed through'. After two or three hours, the group leader might helpfully collapse to the floor and feign death (like the Arnolds) to see if it helped. And anyone who staunchly waved farewell and then, ten minutes later, popped a head round the door to ask 'Was that all right?' would be sent to Coventry forthwith.

Last week, a Durham cricketer's wife visiting her parents in Australia received a rather startling telecommunication from her husband – to wit, a fax informing her that the marriage was over. In terms of goodbyes, it certainly had efficiency to commend it. 'Page 1 of 1', it presumably announced at the top; 'FROM: Graeme Fowler, TO: ex-wife'. But was this act of arm's-length brush-off 'callous and cold', merely? After all, the fax was swift and modern in its brutality, it will fade in time (literally), and mercifully it prevented the cliché marital bust-up which invariably degenerates into scuffle and fisticuffs. To peer and strain even further to see a bright side, at least the cricketer did not line her up on a parade ground and bark, 'All those who are married to me, take one step forward. Where the hell do you think *you're* going, Mrs Fowler?'

Faxes for this purpose are quite rare. The more common goodbye disguises itself, for reasons of humdrum cowardliness, as 'See you later' and 'I'll phone you back'. Last week I moved house – from London to Brighton – but like a genuine spineless dastard I flatly denied its implications on personal relationships to the last. 'So we'll not be seeing you,' London neighbours said. 'Of course you will,' I declared heartily. 'I'll be back, you won't know I've gone, in any case Brighton's not far, just find East Croydon and it's easy.' Why endure the pain and tears (your own, not theirs) when you can avoid it with denial? Personally I have always admired those famous dying words which, instead of solemnly commending the soul to the maker, express 'Much better, thanks; in fact, I fancy I could eat one of Mrs Miggins's meat pies.' H.G. Wells's 'Go away, I'm all right' is a particular favourite, but it runs close with Lord Palmerston's grandiloquent, 'Die, my dear doctor? That's the last thing I shall do.' So when I indulge myself unforgivably by mentioning that this *Times* column will of course continue for ever (and see you next week, and the week after that, phone you later, go away I'm all right), perhaps you will deduce what I'm getting at.

To return to the matter in hand – the Fowler fax – I find that I distrust the temptation to jump to conclusions, to assume it came to Mrs Fowler as a bolt from the sky. It sounds to me more like the act of a desperate person, driven to exasperated lengths. Conceivably, Mr Fowler had been leaving clues for weeks, and had finally exhausted his ingenuity. One remembers the Victoria Wood sketch that went: 'Jeff's gone.' 'For good?' 'Well, he's taken the toolshed.' Mrs Fowler may just have been slow on the uptake. One imagines her wandering through the bare, curtainless house, musing 'Funny, where's Graeme got to?', seemingly blind to the words 'I'm off, then' and 'I mean it' sprayed with paint on the living-room walls.

Personally, the only time I successfully said goodbye – really *felt* it, surrendered to it, explored it – was when my wise Chinese acupuncturist left London for Los Angeles. (I know how this must sound, but I'll carry on anyway.) The point was, we had discussed my attitude to separation trauma, so she helped me face a real goodbye (with her), with an emotional result that was positively startling in its depth and scope. The only trouble was, it made me feel like a character from a Woody Allen movie. 'Why are you sobbing?' my surprised colleagues asked, back at the office. 'Why do you think?' I wailed. 'Because my acupuncturist has left for the Coast!'

Possibly it was the most pure and truthful emotional moment of my life, but in the end it proved limiting, because when she returned last year I couldn't face her, too much salt water having passed under that particular bridge. There is a lesson here, I feel. If only she had left me with 'No, I'll soon be home, Los Angeles isn't far, just find the Great Circle and it's easy,' I would have been back to see her, like a shot, and would now be cheerfully bristling with acupuncture needles like quills upon the fretful porpentine.

⌒

When night falls and she doesn't come in for her tea, I usually start to worry. So I go outside and call for her (the old story), and then feel helpless when she still doesn't come. I tell myself that probably she is 'eating out tonight' – because I know how easily she insinuates herself into other houses, and then cadges a meal by acting weak and pathetic. At the end of such an evening, she will come home to me in a telltale over-excited state, not really interested in food.

Still, I will say this for her: she always makes sure I'm all right. Out comes the tin-opener, and there's half a tin of Felix, a handful of Kitty Crunch for my little jaws to work on, even a tub of Sheba if she's been drinking. But it's not the food I am worried about. It's just that I am only properly happy when I know she is safe indoors, curled up asleep on that warm hairy rug of hers, her ears flicking contentedly as she dreams of Jeff Bridges.

She was thirty-one when I got her. Mangy and with a bit of a whiff, but also affectionate. She took time to settle down, and it was clear she had been badly treated in the past, because her mood swings were abrupt and inscrutable – one minute running about like a maniac, the next flaked out in weird angular poses in random places on the carpet. But gradually I earned her trust (and she learned some basic grooming), and now she has this peculiar habit of rubbing her face against my leg, which is quite pleasant actually, though a bit of a nuisance when you are trying to walk downstairs.

To friends who haven't got one, I always say, 'Get one.' I mean it, no hesitation. Yes, they are selfish. Yes, they moult. Yes, they yowl a bit in the night-time and they make it diffi-cult for you to go on holiday. But they make it up to you in so many ways. For one thing, they can sometimes be persuaded to pose with ribbons around their necks. And for another, they are absolutely fascinating to watch. For example, mine spends hour after hour just staring at a big box in the corner of the living-room, not moving an inch, but silently grinding her teeth and tensing her muscles as if to pounce. I have said it before and I'll say it again: I am convinced they can see things we can't see.

For about three years, actually, I had a pair – a male as well as a female – but the male disappeared one day last summer, as abruptly as he arrived, and I never found out what became of him. Run over, possibly. Or locked in a garage by mistake. The sense of loss was awful (that's the problem with getting too attached). They are so frightfully independent, yet incredibly stupid at the same time, so they run into danger while you sit at home worrying yourself demented.

Anyway, my dilemma was: should I get a new one immediately (friends said, 'Get a younger one this time')? But I was worried how the female would react; she might resent it. Certainly she got a bit thin and straggly when he first disappeared, and clawed at the windows. But now she is back to sleeping twenty hours a day, and quite often buries her face in a bowl of food, so I think she has probably fallen on her feet.

I have had her for six years, and she still surprises me. Her only unacceptable habit is that sometimes during the day she will suddenly drop whatever she is doing, dash for the door and disappear; and then an hour later return with all sorts of inedible rubbish – vegetables, pasta, washing-powder – which she dumps on the doormat, looking pleased with herself. It happens about once a week.

Evidently this is standard behaviour, especially from childless females, and I ought to respond magnanimously to these offerings ('Muesli, how lovely') rather than offend her. But it is so clearly a throwback to some primitive hunting-and-gathering instinct that it unsettles me completely. I just don't like to face up to the fact that, you know, deep down, she's an *animal*. 'Look what I got,' she trills, and starts spreading the stuff on the floor. 'Oh yuk,' I say. 'Why ever did you bring home *yoghurt*?' And I give her one of my looks.

Sorry, there's not much point to this. I just thought I'd fill you in. A couple of years ago, you see, she read a pile of books called things like *Catwatching* and *Do Cats Need Shrinks?* and learned some quasi-scientific nonsense about cat behaviour that has honestly given me the pip. For example, she now believes that in the cat world it is a sign of friendship to narrow your eyes. I ask you. Round eyes means aggression, you see; while slitty eyes means 'I'm just a sweet old pussy-cat and I'm your friend.' Several times a day, then, she catches my eye deliberately and then *squints*. It gives me the screaming ab-dabs.

But on the other hand, how sweet of her to try to get an insight. She read somewhere else that cats respond at some deep atavistic level if you lie on the floor, chest up. So she does this, too, and although I have no idea what atavism is, I certainly appreciate a nice thick warm body to lie on, so I clamber aboard, no problem. And this is how I think I will leave you, actually: with me snoozing happily on my pet.

She is happy, lying here chest up, eyes a-squint, for she is cocooned in the pitiable belief that she is practising cat psychology, when in fact cat psychology is practising on her.

GOING LOCO
Lynne Truss

If there were more than one of you, could you run your life more easily? Belinda Johansson is a freelance critic and novelist trying to have it all and not really coping.

Her house and domestic affairs are in chaos; if only she had a double, she would get so much more done. Deep in research for her *magnum opus* – a definitive account of the *doppelgänger* in classic gothic fiction – she fails to notice the echoes of these ghoulish tales disturbingly close at hand. For not only is the cleaning lady taking over her life, but the identity of her husband, Stefan, is in question. Is he a harmless geneticist from Sweden, or actually a cunning clone? Why is the cleaning lady's previous employer having a breakdown, and what on earth has a rat circus got to do with any of this?

Going Loco is a kaleidoscope in which identities shift with alarming ease, a cautionary tale for dizzying times and, quite simply, the funniest novel you could only ever hope to read about outlandish fish cookery, men in skirts and ... Abba.

'Lynne Truss lets her imagination explode in what can only be described as a riddle devised while coming down off halluci-nogens ... The book sings with glittering prose' – *Time Out*

ISBN 1 86197 733 6

TENNYSON'S GIFT
Lynne Truss

It is July 1864 and the Isle of Wight is buzzing with eccentric
creative types. Tennyson recites poetry to furniture while his
invalid wife hides bad reviews in teapots and buries them
in the garden with a teaspoon. Also at Freshwater Bay are
the creepy Charles Dodgson (aka Lewis Carroll) and Julia
Margaret Cameron, a photographer determined to capture an
image of the bard in a suitably heroic pose. Into this cauldron
of unrequited love and egotism step the acclaimed painter G.
F. Watts and his unlikely 16-year-old actress wife Ellen Terry;
also the American father-and-daughter team of phrenologists,
Lorenzo and Jessie Fowler.

A Carrollian comic novel about mid-Victorian highbrows?
About the ideals of Beauty, Art, Friendship, Gratitude and
Serious Beards? The only wonder is that nobody thought of
it before. Unexpectedly moving and luminously wise, *Tennyson's Gift* is the funniest novel ever written about a nineteenth-
century Poet Laureate.

**'The perfect summer book. No deck-chair will be complete
without it.'** – *Independent*

ISBN 1 86197 713 1

WITH ONE LOUSY FREE PACKET OF SEED
Lynne Truss

Osborne Lonsdale, forty-eight, a down-at-heel journalist mysteriously attractive to women, writes a regular celebrity interview for *Come Into the Garden*. This week his 'Me and My Shed' column will be based on the charming garden outhouse owned by TV sitcom star Angela Farmer. Unbeknown to Osborne, driving down to Devon to interview Angela in her country retreat, the sleepy magazine has been taken over by thrusting new management. Gordon Clarke, a teenage inventor of organic virtual reality programmes, has bought *Come Into the Garden* with the intention of closing it down. So it happens that Osborne's research trip is interrupted by a trainload of anxious hacks from London: Lillian, the neurotic secretary with a mail-sorting phobia; Michelle, the obsessive sub-editor who has a secret crush on Osborne; and Trent Carmichael, crime novelist and bestselling author of *S is for ... Secateurs!* The entire cast converge on Honiton where the stage is set for a saga of misunderstandings.

This is Lynne Truss's debut novel. With it she joined the ranks of the greatest comic writers.

'Lynne Truss has written a perfect comic novel at the first attempt ... a witty, ingenious romp.' – *Daily Telegraph*

ISBN 1 86197 749 2